MISSING
THE CHILD
YOU LOVE

MISSING
THE CHILD
YOU LOVE

Finding Hope in the Midst of Death, Disability or Absence

H. Norman Wright

Regal

For more information and
special offers from Regal Books, email us at
subscribe@regalbooks.com

Published by Regal
From Gospel Light
Ventura, California, U.S.A.
www.regalbooks.com
Printed in the U.S.A.

Library of Congress Cataloging-in-Publication Data
Wright, H. Norman.
Missing the child you love : finding hope in the midst of death, disability or absence /
H. Norman Wright.
pages cm
ISBN 978-0-8307-7023-6 (trade paper)
1. Children—Death—Religious aspects—Christianity. 2. Parents—Religious life.
3. Grief—Religious aspects—Christianity. 4. Bereavement—Religious aspects—
Christianity. I. Title.
BV4907.W75 2014
248.8'66—dc23
2013044389

Rights for publishing this book outside the U.S.A. or in non-English languages are
administered by Gospel Light Worldwide, an international not-for-profit ministry.
For additional information, please visit www.glww.org, email info@glww.org, or write to
Gospel Light Worldwide, 1957 Eastman Avenue, Ventura, CA 93003, U.S.A.
To order copies of this book and other Regal products in bulk quantities,
please contact us at 1-800-446-7735.

Contents

1

The World of Grief

If you are reading this book, you are probably living in a state of grief or would like to be supportive of someone who is living with this constant, unwanted companion. I use the word "constant" to underscore what you will be living with for years; and if you have lost a child, for any reason, it will be for life.

I have lived this experience and have written about it extensively. The content of this chapter, which is foundational to the rest of the book, will reflect much of what I've learned through the years and shared in speaking and in my other writing.

I've repeated thoughts and words. There is a reason for this. The state of grief will make it difficult for you to remember what you've read. So, I will repeat what you need to internalize in this chapter and apply it in different ways according to the loss or the topic discussed. The remainder of the book is newly presented material and will, I hope, be of help to you as well.

Grief: We don't like the meaning of the word or the sound of it, yet it is spoken of many times in the Scriptures:

> I tell you the truth, you will weep and mourn while the world rejoices. You will grieve, but your grief will turn to joy (John 16:20).

> I weep with grief; my heart is heavy with sorrow; encourage and cheer me with your words (Ps. 119:28, *TLB*).

Mourning is part of the experience of grief; it is the process where grief is expressed. It is a natural, God-given process of recovery—His gift to us to help get us through the pain. Anyone who experiences loss experiences grief. Mourning, however, is a choice. One cannot make grief better, make it go away, fix it or just "get over it."

People have created many word pictures to describe the experience of grief. Often when those who grieve read these words, they say, "Yes. That's exactly the way I feel. I thought I was the only one." They realize they are not alone—that what they are experiencing is normal grief.

One grieving father said:

> Grief is like a wave. It comes rolling in from a far-off place. I could no more push it back than if I were standing in the water at the beach. I could not fight the wave. It moved over me and under me and broke against me, but I could never stop it. It arrived at its destination. It worked around me. The harder I fought it, the more exhausted I became. So it is with grief. If I tried to fight it, it would vanquish me. If I pushed it down it would stick in my soul and emerge as something else; depression, bitterness, exhaustion. If I yielded to the waves and let it carry me, however, it would take me to a new place.[1]

Grief takes you to the top of the waves, and when the waves break, you struggle in the froth of emotion. Grief brings memories and will expose who you really are inside. As the waves move closer to the shore, their power gets spent and they slowly bubble up to the edge of the sand. The more you stand and fight and rail against the waves, the more exhausted you become. It is an exercise in futility. But the more you accept them, hold out your arms to them and even embrace them, the sooner you will recover. You need to take a step that for many is difficult—you need to yield to the grief. You need to let it do its work in your life through mourning.

When you enter into grief, you've entered into the valley of shadows. There is nothing heroic or noble about grief. It's painful. It's work. It's a lingering process. But it is necessary for all kinds of losses. Grief has been labeled everything from intense mental anguish to acute sorrow and even deep remorse.

> When our child dies, it hurts more than anything we can imagine. In the beginning of grief, we are destitute because we can't know that the pain will end. Certainly, there is no assurance that it will ever end.
>
> But it does. We have to learn much along the way before we can move through the process. We must learn patience, the value of change, the beauty of simplicity, the importance of laughter, the life-sustaining strength of relationships, and the joy of spontaneity and adventure. We have to remind ourselves that, deep down, each of us is a child that must be nurtured.
>
> Probably grief's most important lesson is faith—faith that, even in the blackest moments of despair, a clearing will appear somewhere up ahead. There will be better times— they do come. I can promise you that they will.[2]

Many of us have joined a club before, but there is one club no one wants to join.

> The membership requirements of this club are anything but enviable. You have to have felt the floor dropping out and the sky falling in, all in one awful, unthinkable day. You have to have wondered whether you would be able to figure out which shoe to put on which foot, and then wondered why you should bother anyway. You have to have cringed, and perhaps silently flared, when all those people who meant so well said such incredibly inappropriate things to you. You have to have believed you were the first person in the history of the planet to feel so empty.
>
> And then later, you find out that other people have felt this way, too. You find out that they have survived, but that they—like you—have survived only as changed people.
>
> Like you, they know there's no going back. You may look exactly like the old you, but you're a different person now. Grief of this magnitude changes you.[3]

There are a multitude of emotions involved in the grief process—emotions that seem out of control and often appear in conflict with one another. With each loss may come bitterness, emptiness, apathy, love, anger, guilt, sadness, fear, self-pity and a feeling of helplessness.

Connecting the Pieces

Experiencing the process can be likened to putting a complex puzzle together. There are as many ways to put the pieces together as there are individuals doing it. However, there *are* designated puzzle pieces that fit in specific relationship to others. Only when the puzzle is complete can a person sit back and appreciate the entire picture for what it is and declare it finished. That is also true of the grief process; it is an individual journey, yet there are five specific tasks with corresponding behaviors to address to help you move through your grief detour.

Acceptance
There are certain tasks to accomplish in grief.

First, you need to accept the reality that your loved one has died and is unable to return. This may seem obvious, but emotionally accepting the reality of the death can be a tremendous challenge.

Expression
Second, you need to express all of your emotions associated with the death. Keeping emotions bottled up inside can complicate your grief journey.

Memory Storage
Third, you need to sort through and identify memories of your loved one and find a place to store them so you can begin to move on. This task basically means that because your loved one is no longer present—is no longer a dynamic and active part of your ongoing journey—you need to make him or her a vital and rich memory of your life.

Identity
Fourth, you need to identify who you are—independent of your deceased loved one. Reworking your sense of identity is a critical aspect of your grief journey.

Investment

Finally, you begin to reinvest in your life a way that is consistent with your reshaped sense of identity—determining your own personal interests and desires at this point in your life.[4] This may not be easy.

Elemental Drives

There are also five cries you will experience that the author of the book *The Five Cries of Grief* describes.

"I Hurt . . ."

There is a *cry of pain* that can bring you to your knees. For many, it's as if something has been wrenched or torn out of them. This pain can reside within the body as well as within the emotions. It will come and go, often for years, and for no apparent reason.

As one father wrote about the loss of his son:

> The intensity of pain will diminish, but the loss haunts us to the end. But since loss and grief are a part of life, strangely enough the sorrow becomes a kind of minor chord along with the jubilant majors to give life a new richness. It would be far more difficult if we could not believe that our sons are a part of that great bleacher company, the cloud of witnesses, now cheering us on from the other side.[5]

Another parent said:

> The sky had fallen upon my world and there was no comfort to be found. I slumped to my knees beside my bed, and then lay facedown on the beige carpeting. In the dark silence, I waited for my family to arrive.
>
> I was screaming inside, but I couldn't speak. I was disoriented, my mind invisibly suspended upon my black pit of grief. I couldn't pray, I couldn't think.
>
> I didn't know it then, but I was experiencing the first waves of shock. Wave after wave hit, intermittently, jarring me against the reality of what had happened, and then

plunged me into the depths of indescribable pain. I fought against the facts, the fear.[6]

The pain of grief can feel overwhelming. Pain is a companion to grief and can feel like a visitor that has long overstayed its welcome. No one is immune to pain, but everyone resists its intrusion.

There are several ways people attempt to resist the pain. Some fight it through denial. They attempt to live their lives as though nothing has happened. When they hear about the death, their first response is often, "No, that's not true." "Tell me it isn't so!" "You're mistaken." They're trying to absorb the news, but it takes time to filter the shock. This *is* normal.

The author of *A Grace Disguised* wrote, "Ultimately it [denial] diminishes the capacity of their souls to grow bigger in response to pain."[7]

Denial serves as emotional anesthesia and a defense mechanism so that you will not be totally overwhelmed by the loss. Denial allows you to gradually comprehend the loss, which makes it more bearable.

Grief moves through several levels of denial. Each stage painfully brings home the reality of the loss a bit deeper. In that first stage is accepting it in our heads; then in our feelings; and finally, we adjust life's pattern to reflect the reality of what has occurred.

There is a price to pay for prolonged denial. The amount of energy required to keep denial operating drains us, and in time, we can become damaged emotionally, delaying our recovery.

Denial blocks out the unthinkable and brings with it fear of the unknown, since it keeps away the reality of what happened. As denial lessens, the pain begins to settle in; as it does, fear of the unknown diminishes. Denial is like a cushion that slowly gets pulled out from under us. By the time it is gone, we are ready to consider the hard reality, at least in private.

So often, when a child dies, a family feels compelled to try to bury the sadness along with the child. Officially, anyway, the sorrow becomes a secret. Social pressures conspire to make it less harrowing to avoid the discussion

entirely rather than to face the questions or the judg-
ments—real or imagined—that accompany a child's death.

So for some parents, a child's death is best stuffed
away in a safe spot for hiding, a place that only they can
visit.[8]

"I Want . . ."

There is also a *cry of longing*—this comes from the sense of emptiness and loneliness that exists because of the loss of a loved one.
For many this is a longing they've never experienced before. It can
occur at a special time of the year or when certain events occur,
or for no apparent reason. For some, wherever they go, even if it's
enjoyable, there is the feeling of "I wish he (or she) were here."
The longing may come out in cries of "Where are you?" "Why did
you leave?" "Why now?" There's an intense desire to see and hear
the loved one again.

"I Need . . ."

A third cry is for *supportive love*. One of the worst experiences is to
feel that you are alone, isolated in a world full of people. Those
in grief have some specific needs for love and support. They need
family members to support them, especially those who are healthy
emotionally and can give encouragement. They also need others
who accept what has happened, who care and who can help with
what needs to be done in terms of daily tasks. They need people to
reach out in the coming months and years with care and concern.
They need others to talk about the deceased, share memories and
use the deceased person's name. Continuous support and love is
a priority.

"I Don't Understand"

William Barclay said, "The hardest lesson of all . . . is to accept what
one cannot understand and still say, 'God, thou art love. I build
my faith on that.'"[9] This is a cry to accept what has happened,
but often the desire to comprehend is overwhelmed. Often one's
relationship with God becomes disrupted for a while. For many,
their desire is to try to make time stand still, to keep things as they
were, to return to a previous time.

As one grieving father shared:

I was bothered by seemingly contradictory emotions. How could I laugh when I was feeling so sad? How could I be resentful of what happened and yet accept it? How could I let go and still hang on? How could I believe and doubt in the same breath? How could I actually experience deep joy, and yet feel the unutterable pain of having lost?

The *cry of why* is the cry of lament. This cry is good. It is necessary. It is a cry of protest to God, but also a cry of faith. Michael Card's book *A Sacred Sorrow* describes how lament is a biblical pattern for our lives:

Why then, does God enshrine so many laments in His Word? Laments, we must realize, *are* God's Word. Why are so many biblical characters shown as disappointed and angry with God? Do we seek to learn from all the other facets of their lives but this? I would put it to you this way. People like Job, David, Jeremiah and even Jesus reveal to us that prayers of complaint can still be prayers of faith.[10]

He also talks about the purpose of lamenting:

What lament would have us understand is that the answer is being graciously given. His Presence is always with us. Lament is the path that takes us to the place where we discover that there is no complete answer to pain and suffering, only Presence. Our questions and complaints will never find individual answers (even Job's questions were never fully answered). The only Answer is the dangerous, disturbing, comforting Presence, which is the true answer to all our questions and hopes.[11]

"What Does It All Mean?"

A final cry is the *cry for significance*, the desire to see something good eventually come out of this loss. It's the process of transforming grief into growth.[12]

Grieving is a matter of beginning with the question "Why did this happen to me?" and eventually moving on to "How can I learn through this experience?" "How can I now go on with my life?" When the *how* question replaces the *why* question, one has started to live with the reality of the loss. *Why* questions reflect a search for meaning and purpose in loss. *How* questions reflect searching for ways to adjust to the loss.[13]

The eventual goal is to be able to say, "This loss I've experienced is a crucial upset in my life. In fact, it is the worst thing that will ever happen to me. But is it the end of my life? No. I can still have a rich, fulfilling life. Grief has been my companion and has taught me much. I can use it to grow into a stronger person than I was before my loss."

But to be able to say this takes more time than most of us understand.

Grieving is a disorderly process. It can't be controlled or scheduled. Grief will take the shape of a spiral figure rather than a linear one. Grief is not a straight line moving forward only to return you to where you used to be. A person may think he or she has left behind that intense pain only to discover the sense of relief recurs over and over again as pain comes close and then moves away again, for a time.

Grief disrupts your mind and your thinking ability. Confusion moves in and memory takes a vacation. If you suffer short-term memory loss after a death, it's probably a result of the stress and anxiety you are experiencing. Your life has been paralyzed and shut down. The more you accept what is occurring, the sooner it will pass.

You may even experience your last interaction with your deceased child. Some say that the experience is so real it's as though they are actually there talking with the deceased person again. These experiences will pass. They're normal responses to what has occurred.

You may be easily distracted and perhaps disoriented, even if you're usually decisive. Now you may be afraid to make choices.

Many people find that their sense of time is distorted. Time goes too fast or too slowly. Past and future collapse together. A clock can be sitting in front of their face but it doesn't register.

Recently, a grieving mother said she was in a time warp, frozen in time.

Grief is one of the most uncomfortable places you will ever live. It hurts, confuses, upsets and frightens anyone who is living with it.

Whenever there is loss, there will be grief. But some do not grieve or mourn. Some make a choice not to express all the feelings inside, so their grief gets accumulated. Saving it up won't lessen the pain; it will only intensify it. Silence covers a wound before the cleansing has occurred. The result turns into an emotional infection. Perhaps you, or a family member, have experienced this.

Some people try to make others carry their burden. But grief can't be shared. Everyone has to carry it alone and in his or her own way.[14]

Grief is slow, and it needs to be slow, even though most people probably want to rush it along. It will take longer than anyone has patience for. Although time seems to stand still, especially at night, the slowness of grief is necessary.

Each person grieves and heals differently. You may want to be connected to people as much as possible, or you may prefer to be left alone. Some prefer to take care of their own problems, while others want assistance. One prefers activity, while another prefers just the opposite. Others may attempt to fill their lives with what they don't want.

Even though it will take effort, you may need to let others know what you need and what is the best way for them to help you. When grief becomes your close companion, you will experience it in many ways. It will permeate and change feelings, thoughts and attitudes.

This chapter is only an introduction to your grieving journey. Where did you see yourself in the chapter? Perhaps it's time to set the book aside and reflect on what you've read. You may even want to reread the chapter before proceeding.

2

The Need to Grieve

There are several factors to keep in mind that may ease some of the pressure you put on yourself to understand your grief.

First of all, even though grief is as normal as the common cold, it's not an illness that needs a prescription or surgery. Each person expresses grief differently, and there isn't one right way to grieve. So never compare your way of grieving with that of others, for yours is uniquely your own.

Your grief schedule will be your own. It will take as long as it takes, and that, too, is normal. Don't listen to the admonitions or advice of others, for they don't know how long your grieving will (or needs to) last.

The loss you now grieve is not your only loss. Each new loss creates additional or secondary losses to identify and confront. When you lose a family member, often the losses seem to multiply, and you wonder, *Will this ever end?*

With each new loss, you may go through the same thing you felt in a previous loss of a loved one, even though you thought you had completed your grieving. It's not at all unusual for old grief to mingle with current grief.[1] The author of *Unspeakable Losses* explains it this way:

> Losses never stand alone. New losses reverberate with the memories of old ones, bringing a new significance to each. We are constantly trying to make sense of our experiences

to make our lives coherent, to make what happens to us meaningful. When sudden unexpected losses occur, we have to struggle to make sense of them. They can threaten to overwhelm us with a sense of our own impatience until we come up with an explanation for why they occurred and how we can avoid having them happen to us again.[2]

We want others to accept and understand where we are in our grief and to not try to fix us, for we don't need to be fixed. We're not broken. When we're sad we want to know it's all right.

Do you need to hear that sorrow is not your enemy? It's true. Your grief keeps you close to the one you lost. And if you've lost a close loved one, isn't he or she worthy of sorrow? Your feelings will fluctuate, and there will be a time for laughter, which is appropriate. Nancy Guthrie, in on one of her books, wrote:

> Sometimes we are afraid to laugh lest people think our pain has passed or that our sorrow has been a sham. But just as tears give vent to the deep sorrow we feel, laughter reveals that while grief may have a grip on us, it hasn't choked the life out of us.
>
> Laughter takes some of the sting out of hurt. It gives us perspective and relieves the pressure.[3]

What are some other normal behaviors? Do you find yourself not wanting to interact with others? It's all right to want to be alone, and others don't have to understand. Often we need to be alone with our grief. But it's also all right to want to be with others, especially if you were involved as a caregiver for a period of time. You may need the comfort and support, or just the presence, of others. Often, another person will help by listening or sharing his or her own memories. But it's also all right not to talk about the deceased, and to engage in discussions of anything else you would like to talk about.

When you are in grief, your vulnerability and greatest weakness may rise to the surface. You're not your usual self—you can't be and won't be. Just assert this and lean upon others and the Lord. He will be your main source of joy, as well as your strength.

There will be days when you will surprise yourself by your strength and stability. Just remember that this doesn't mean your grief is over. It's just a break, and your feelings of grief will return. So, when someone asks how you're doing, you have a wide variety of possible responses. And all of these are your responses. This is you in grief, and you can be free to share what you are feeling with others.[4] Author Susan Duke shares this insight:

> I quickly learned that putting on a good face doesn't matter when you can't stop your heart from breaking, and that people can respond only to what they see. I couldn't expect people to know if I was having a bad day if I pretended to be okay.[5]

One mother said that when she was asked how she was doing, she stopped saying, "I'm fine" each time she was asked. Her truthful replies became: "It's tough, but I'm hanging in there." "I'm hoping tomorrow will be a better day."[6]

Long recovery does not mean you did or didn't love as much as you thought you did. You will react to grief and recover from grief just like you react to all other things in life. You have your own timetable.

Most likely, recovery and readiness to move on will take years. With the loss of a child, 5 to 10 years is not unusual. But there is no set timetable for the recovery.

Does grief really have an end in sight? Perhaps. But the timeframe can be limitless. There is no way to determine a precise amount of time to recovery.

For many, the word "recovery" implies that grief is an illness, which it is not. Another issue is that people may not give you the time to recover; and you may not give yourself time to recover. *You* may be the source of the greatest amount of pressure. You may be the one who feels that your faith is not strong if you are not well in a period of weeks. It may be you who tries to send your grief away.

Grief Recovery's ICU

When you're in grief, you're in one of the most painful experiences of your life. Grief will leave you feeling vulnerable, exhausted and weak.

Your best response is to treat yourself as if you were in intensive care. Your focus is upon yourself. You need to care for yourself, and that is not selfish. Grieving is a time of convalescence.

Give Yourself Permission

You need to give yourself permission to grieve. You will grieve whether or not you give yourself permission, but the difference is that if you do not give yourself permission, you will be in a state of internal war during the grieving process. If you do give yourself permission, you can relax and not fight against yourself or the process.

To fight against yourself adds tension and hurt to the grief. It diminishes the energy you so desperately need in grief recovery. To fight against yourself can lead you to act like you are well long before you are. Acting as if you are well will only lengthen the grief process. And you may, as a result, relapse later when the energy drain of acting well gets to be too much to bear.

How do you give yourself permission to grieve? By recognizing the need for grieving. It is the natural way of working through the loss of a love. Grieving is not weakness or absence of faith. It is as natural as crying when you hurt, sleeping when you are tired, or sneezing when your nose itches. It is nature's way of healing a broken heart.

In her book *How to Survive the Loss of a Child,* Catherine Sanders wrote:

> The lessons of grief can help us build an inner stability and strength so that, when we are confronted with adversity again, we will know, without a shadow of a doubt, it isn't that loss comes only to teach us. That would be cruel indeed. It is, instead, that when we suffer a loss, we are given the opportunity to open ourselves to change. And it is in our willingness to accept the changes, even embrace them, that the greatest growth is made possible. . . . The best response for you at this time is to treat yourself as if you were in intensive care. Your focus is upon yourself and no one else. You need to care for yourself and that is not selfish. Grieving is a time of convalescence.[7]

Grief is not an enemy; it is a friend. It is the natural process of walking through hurt and growing because of the walk. Let it happen.

Stand up tall to friends and to yourself and say, "Don't take my grief away from me. I deserve it, and I am going to have it."[8]

The Necessity of Saying No

This suggestion may sound strange, but it's all right for you to practice saying no to others. Many are going to try to fix you, but you don't need to be fixed since you're not broken. Some are going to be impatient with your grieving journey. You are not grieving for anyone else to feel comfortable. It's not for their benefit, but for yours. When you hear advice or suggestions or requests from others, just say you need to think about it and you will let them know. It's a polite way of saying no.

You don't need to be concerned about hurting someone else at this time. The other individual may be grieving for the same person you lost, but the one you need to take care of now is you. You probably don't even have enough energy for that. If you've been the one others have always leaned on, this will be a big adjustment for them, but a necessary one. You may be the one who needs help now. But consider carefully the offers of help. Sometimes you end up feeling drained rather than replenished.

To reduce the pressure of having to explain to others what you are experiencing, you may want to print a card or letter to give out when others ask, and post it on Facebook.

The Necessity of Healing Sleep

Sleep can be difficult when you're grieving. But sleep is essential, for the less sleep you have, the more difficulty you will have with your emotions. They will rage out of control. Here are a few suggestions that have worked for many.

Some people want to dream about their loved one, while others do not. Most would like to remember their dreams. If so, you may want to keep a dream journal. As soon as you wake up, spend a few minutes writing down what you can remember. Do this before you get out of bed. Start with any fragment of the dream and then try to reconstruct it. Keep a pad of paper and pen by your bed and remind yourself that you will remember your dreams.

If you have repetitive nightmares, prior to going to sleep recall the details of the nightmare and change the ending to one that is positive. Write it out and read it out loud. This suggestion has been helpful to many.

The Necessity of Reliance on God

If you are struggling with falling asleep, or you wake up and have difficulty getting back to sleep, read the following Scriptures aloud and pray them just before you turn out the light:

> When you lie down, you shall not be afraid; yes, you shall lie down and your sleep shall be sweet. Be not afraid of sudden terror *and* panic, nor of the stormy blast *or* the storm and ruin of the wicked when it comes [for you will be guiltless], For the Lord shall be your confidence, firm *and* strong, and shall keep your foot from being caught [in a trap or hidden danger] (Prov. 3:24-26, *AMP*).

> You will not be afraid when you go to bed, and you will sleep soundly through the night (Prov. 3:24, *GNB*).

> If I'm sleepless at midnight, I spend the hours in grateful reflection (Ps. 63:6, *THE MESSAGE*).

> When my anxious thoughts multiply within me, Your consolations delight my soul (Ps. 94:19, *NASB*).

> I will lie down and sleep in peace, for you alone, O LORD, make me dwell in safety (Ps. 4:8).

> Do not be afraid of the terror by night (Ps. 91:5, *NASB*).

> In a dream, a vision of the night, when sound sleep falls on men . . . then He opens the ears of men, and seals their instruction (Job 33:15-16, *NASB*).

> Dear God,
> We give thanks for the darkness of the night where lies the world of dreams. Guide us closer to our dreams so that we may be nourished by them. Give us good dreams

and memory of them so that we may carry their poetry and mystery into our daily lives

Grant us deep and restful sleep that we may wake refreshed with strength enough to renew a world grown tired.

We give thanks for the inspiration of stars, the dignity of the moon and the lullabies of crickets and frogs.

Let us restore the night and reclaim it as a sanctuary of peace, where silence shall be music to our hearts and darkness shall throw light upon our souls. Good night. Sweet dreams. Amen.[9]

As we conclude this chapter, consider these words from the author of *Grieving Forward*:

In the soft glow of my bedroom cathedral, I felt God's presence. I envisioned His tears . . . and I believed "the Lord . . . heard the voice of my weeping" (Ps. 6:8, *NASB*).

That God knew—that He had heard—even when I couldn't hear Him, became my center of hope during the first painful hours of my grief. Through the presence of those who loved me and shared my pain. He comforted. Through intermingled tears, He ministered compassion and love.

I learned early on that isolating myself was not the answer. The voice of darkness is always loudest when you are alone. When I couldn't verbalize my pain and devastation, Kelly's words, "We're going to be okay," made me believe, at least for the moment that somehow in a way I couldn't yet comprehend, we would.

If you are experiencing the shock and disbelief of fresh grief, remember that God hears the voice of your weeping, He uses the presence and words of family and friends who simply express "I'm here" to pierce the darkness beneath your fallen sky and give you a glimpse of tomorrow's light.

God will bring me out of my darkness into the light, and I will see his goodness. Then my enemy will see that God is for me and be ashamed for taunting me, "Where is that God of yours?" (Mic. 7:9-10, *TLB*).[10]

RECOMMENDED READING

- Lynn Eib, *When God and Grief Meet*
- Nancy Guthrie, *Hearing Jesus Speak to Your Sorrow*
- H. Norman Wright, *Experiencing Grief*

3

The Faces and Feelings of Grief

Why does everyone have to go through the complexities and pain of grief? What is the purpose of grief?

- Through grief you express your feelings about your loss.
- Through grief you express your protest at the loss, as well as your desire to change what happened and have it not be true. This is a normal response.
- Through grief you express the effects you have experienced from the devastating impact of the loss.[1]
- Through grief you may experience God in a new way that changes your life. As Job said, "My ears had heard of you before, but now my eyes have seen you" (Job 42:5, NCV).

During seasons of grief, the days may seem like night, often with a blanket of fog drifting around you. The psalmist reflected this when he said, "When my spirit was overwhelmed within me . . ." (Ps. 142:3, KJV). These words literally mean, "the muffling of my spirit." As your grief clears, you will find the sun breaking through your gloom. The psalmist said, "Weeping may remain for a night, but rejoicing comes in the morning" (Ps. 30:5).

Perhaps one of the best descriptions of grief comes from Joanne T. Jozefowski's book *The Phoenix Phenomenon: Rising from the Ashes of*

Grief. These characteristics, or symptoms, with such a fitting title, seem to resonate with almost everyone I've shared them with and, all too often, I hear, "Yes. Every one of these symptoms describes what my life is like right now."

These "crazy" feelings of grief are actually a sane response to grief:

- distorted thinking patterns, "crazy" and/or irrational thoughts, fearful thoughts
- feelings of despair and hopelessness
- out-of-control or numbed emotions
- changes in sensory perceptions (sight, taste, smell, and so on)
- increased irritability
- may want to talk a lot or not at all
- memory lags and mental "short-circuiting"
- inability to concentrate
- obsessive focus on the loved one
- lose track of time
- increase or decrease of appetite and/or sexual desire
- difficulty falling or staying asleep
- dreams in which the deceased seems to visit the griever
- nightmares in which death themes are repeated
- physical illness like the flu, headaches or other maladies
- shattered beliefs about life, the world and even God

The passage of grief will take longer than one could ever imagine. It tends to intensify at three months, and on special dates and the one-year anniversary.[2]

Through Flickering Light and Shadow

Grief takes on many characteristics: disruption, gaps, holes, confusion. It disrupts one's entire life schedule, and the ensuing grief doesn't leave one particle of life untouched. It's all consuming. There are body changes. Food doesn't taste the same, nor will the fragrance of a favorite flower be as intense. The frequency of tears clouds vision. Some people experience a tightness of breath or rapid heart rate. Eating and sleeping patterns change. Some people will sleep and sleep, while others wish sleep would come. Sleep is either an easy escape or it's elusive. Dreams or nightmares occur. These disruptions will decrease in time, but recovery is not a smooth, straightforward path; it's a forward-backward dance.

Diminished Identity

If grief occurs because of the loss of your child, your life has now been divided into two segments—life before the death and life after the death. As well, grief can bring out the best or the worst in a person.

Prior to your loss, life was going in a well-established direction. There was an identity attached to the one you have lost. You are no longer exactly who you were. The person who died was part of your identity. He or she was someone's mother or aunt or spouse or brother. He or she continues to be that person in your heart and memory, but there's a vacant place where the loved one stood. The loss of this person has subtracted part of who you were.

Sensory Overload

You may also experience the "face in the crowd" syndrome. You think you have seen the one you lost or you have heard his or her voice, or smelled his or her perfume or cologne. This can happen at home or in public places. You may wake up at night and swear you sensed your loved one's presence in the room or heard him or her call your name. You think you're going crazy and hesitate to share the experience with others for fear of what they will think. This experience is more common than most realize and can last for as long as 18 months.

Heightened Sense of Loss

It is not just the loss of the loved one that is so painful. It is also the other losses that occur because of the one who has died: the way he or she lived, loved, slept, ate, worked and worshiped—all are gone from your experience of earthly life. Often the death of the loved one brings up not just grief for what has been lost, but also grief for what he or she never had and never will have.

There is a loss of the present as well as the future. This especially impacts relationships. You may feel awkward around others for whom the one lost was also a loved one. A death can either put distance in a relationship or draw it together and connect in a greater intimacy than before. Death can be a wedge or a source of confusion. You may feel disconnected with others, alienated, and you may tend to withdraw, which reinforces your feelings. This can lead to a belief that "others just don't understand," which is often true.

Learning to Accept What Is

The process of grief involves saying goodbye to the old life. This occurs with the acknowledgment that the loved one is truly gone and won't return. Many struggle with holding on while trying to let go. The ongoing task is to develop a new way of relating to the one who died.

Sometime, you may wish you could communicate with your loved one again. One of the steps toward learning to accept what is comes when you say goodbye to your child and share with him or her what you wanted to say in life and perhaps didn't get to do.

Another step in accepting what is comes in acknowledging the inevitable behavior changes. You may say, "I'm just not myself." That's true. You won't be for some time. You may find yourself zoning out when others are talking; your mind drifts off because it's difficult to stay focused and attentive. You feel detached from people and activities even though they're an important part of your life. What is upsetting to many experiencing grief is how absent-minded one becomes. You may cry for "no apparent" reason. It is common to lose your sense of awareness of where you are, relating both to time and place.

Nature's Protection

Whether the death was expected or sudden, you may experience numbness. The more unexpected and traumatic the loss, the more intense the numbness will be. At first, feelings are muted, like muting the sound on a TV. The initial shock of knowing a loved one is dead puts most people into a paralyzing state of shock. This is a period when no one in grief can describe things clearly, thanks to nature's protective measures. Shock is a natural protection, as though someone has given you anesthesia. It insulates you from the intensity of feelings of loss, but it also may prevent you from understanding the full experience of the loss.

After the Numbness Wears Off

There will be a time when feelings could be described as a time of suffering and disorganization, or even chaos. The trance is over. You talk about scenes rather than stages. And there are those who bypass some scenes. After the numbness wears off, the pain of separation comes. Sometimes those who grieve wish they could go back to the initial stage of numbness or shock. At least there the pain wasn't so intense.

There is an intense longing for the return of the person who was lost—for the sight of them, the sound of them, their smell and just knowing he or she could walk through the door again. One author described the loss of a loved one as "like having a tree that has been growing in one's heart yanked out by its roots, leaving a gaping hole or wound."[3] And the question begins to form, "Why?" Perhaps you've done that.

You may ask or even shout "Why?" countless times a day at this point. Many wonder, *Do I have the right to ask why?* It's not just a question; it's a heart-wrenching cry of protest. It's the reaction of "No, this shouldn't be! It isn't right!"

Job, in the Bible, asked the why question 16 times. And there are others. Listen to their cries:

Why, O LORD, do you stand far off? Why do you hide yourself in times of trouble? (Ps. 10:1).

How long, O LORD ? Will you forget me forever? How long will you hide your face from me? How long must I wrestle with my thoughts and every day have sorrow in my heart? How long will my enemy triumph over me? (Ps. 13:1-2).

Ken Gire wrote, "Painful questions, all of them. Unanswered questions, many of them. And if we live long enough and honestly enough, one day we will ask them, too."[4]

It's not unusual to struggle to pray. At times it's as though the words stick in your mind and can't get past your lips. The questions, concerns, pleas and requests are there, but they derail when you attempt to express them to God.

Grief's Clusters of Feelings

What lies ahead? You will experience a variety of feelings and emotions, some of which hang out together and seem to visit you as a group. One of the clusters of feelings to emerge will be a sense of emptiness, loneliness and isolation, even when others are next to you in your grief. Invisible boundaries have been erected. In two or three months' time, there will be even more loneliness and isolation as friends and family start to pull away from you. It is a natural happening because they are moving into all the daily issues of life and are no longer focusing as much on the loss.

Feelings Connected with Lack of Control

The second common cluster of feelings is fear and anxiety; and the fears accumulate. They may come and go or become a constant sense of dread. Fear and anxiety are common responses whenever we face the unknown and the unfamiliar. These feelings range from the fear of being alone to fear of the future, additional loss, desertion or abandonment.

Fear works as an alarm system that warns us of major changes in our understanding and assumptions regarding self and others.[5] Anxiety awakens an awareness of a person's inability to control events. You may feel that you should have been able to prevent or at least predict the occurrence of the loss. "What will I do?" is a phrase that expresses fear. The greater the emotional investment in the one who was lost, the more one will tend to feel like a ship adrift at sea.

You may fear that if you stop wanting your child to return, it means you have stopped loving him or her. In addition, the worst agony of intense grief occurs when you realize the return you want more than anything else is the one you can't have.[6]

Some have said, "You need to let go of the loved one completely." But consider the thinking of the author of *The Heart of Grief*:

> Grieving persons who want their loved ones back need to look for some other way to love them while they are apart.

Desperate longing prevents their finding that different way of loving. Letting go of having them with us in the flesh is painful and necessary. But it is not the same as completely letting go. We still hold the gifts they gave us, the value and meaning we found in their lives. We can love them as we cherish their memories. We can love them as we treasure their legacies in our practical lives, and spirits. But there is nothing in all of this that implies that we must let go completely. There is no reason to let go of the good with the bad.[7]

You may wake up and ask, "How can I face the day without him (without her)?" You are afraid of being on your own. You may be anxious over dealing with the pain of the separation. You may be upset over the realization that you are a different person. You're "without" someone. You may worry over how other family members will cope and survive. Since you've lost one person, what if you lose another family member or friend, especially if the current loss was sudden and unexpected?

Feelings Connected with Unrealistic Expectations

Guilt and shame walk their way into the grief process. There are numerous sources for the guilt. The most immediate guilt comes from taking some responsibility for the loss, or perhaps connecting it to a discussion one feels contributed to the loss in some way. Guilt is possibly the most difficult emotion to handle. It's often tied into unrealistic expectations. Some parents hold themselves responsible for events over which they had no control, such as thinking they could have done something different or done something more in order to prevent the death. Guilt could also be left-over unfinished business they wish they had attended to, and it leads to regret that turns into guilt.

Some continue to live in the land of regret and let their lives become a continuous self-recriminating statement. And the regrets seem to grow: "I should have said . . ." "I should have done . . ." "I should have known . . ."

Guilt may result from unresolved negative feelings over things a person did or didn't do. It's common in the early phases of grief to recall all that was negative in a relationship while failing to remember the positives equally as well. Another tendency is to dwell on all the bad or negative things a person thinks he or she did in the relationship with the person he or she lost while over-focusing on all the good things the deceased did. And then there is survivor guilt. The person in grief feels guilty because he or she is still alive.

Guilt is an unpredictable emotion, and that by itself creates guilt. Some experience guilt because they're not recovering according to their expected timetable. This is where "should" and "if only" come to mind. If a death is unexpected or comes sooner than anticipated, a tendency to blame self rushes to the forefront. After we've blamed others, it's easy to transfer blame to ourselves. "If only I had . . ." The list is endless.

Some imagine that if they had done something differently they could have prevented the death. This feeling could overwhelm if suicide was the cause of a loved one's death.

Feelings Connected with a Sense of Unfairness

A feeling of anger is a feeling of displeasure, irritation and protest. When in grief, anger is often a protest, a desire to make someone pay, to declare the unfairness of the death when frustrated, hurt, afraid or feeling helpless. Anger/hostility acts as a protective self-defense emotion that demands the world be predictable and operate according to one's sense off fairness. Sometimes the anger is expressed like a heat-seeking missile. It can erupt suddenly without warning.

Anger is a response to hurt or pain. The pain can come from the past, the present or the future. When the pain comes from the past, the predominant feeling is resentment. It's not uncommon to experience these feelings even toward the one who died. When direct expression gets blocked, it leaks out and gets invested elsewhere. If it is invested against oneself, it can turn into depression.

It may be especially hard for some people to admit being angry at God, perhaps for not responding in the way the person wanted; or angry because their faith and beliefs didn't seem to work. This kind of distress over the failure of God to respond in a desired way can prolong the grief process.

Feelings Connected with Inaccurate Perception

Finally, there is a cluster of feelings named sadness, depression and despair. Depression makes each day look as though the dark clouds are here to stay. Apathy blankets the person like a shroud, and withdrawal becomes a lifestyle. When depression hits, accurate perspective leaves. A person's depression will alter relationships because of oversensitivity to what others say and do. Jeremiah the prophet displayed these feelings: "Desperate is my wound. My grief is great. My sickness is incurable, but I must bear it" (Jer. 10:19, *TLB*). The deeper the depression the more paralyzing the sense of helplessness is. Depression can also affect us spiritually and change the way we see God.

Some have said that grief is the blackout night of confusion because of all the emotions. The range of feelings is like a smorgasbord. Each day there's a wide variety to choose from. There will be daily variations of emotions that come and go. Just when you think they're gone for good, they come again and overlap one another. Over time these emotions come less frequently and less intensely.

Your Feelings Are Normal

One of the struggles of grief is wondering if it's all right to feel and think what you are feeling and thinking. You know what you're experiencing, but you wonder if it's okay, and you hope it is okay with those around you. One of the secret feelings of grief is relief. Few would admit to this. It's an "I shouldn't be experiencing this" feeling.

This is where the Ball of Grief is so helpful (see following page). To assist you in identifying your emotions, look at this ball of grief each day to see where you are, since feelings come and go. It may help to share this graphic with others and talk about your feelings together.

It's true that we can hold back and bottle up feelings, but not for long. If we don't let them out, we'll discover they will find their own means of expression.

Ball of Grief

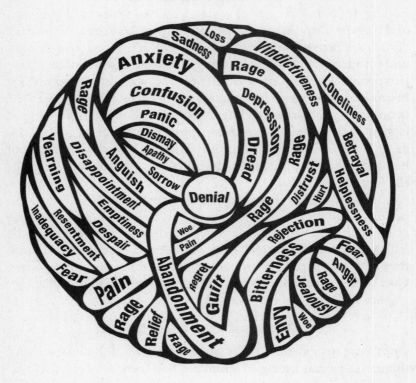

4

The Death of a Child

When our 22-year-old son, Matthew, died, we weren't expecting it, at least not right away. But as time went on, we began to wonder. He had been struggling for months with reflux-esophagitis—a burning of the lining of the esophagus. So he went in for surgery. These are the words of our experience, expressed by Matthew's mother, Joyce.

The operation appeared to go all right, although the esophagus was thin as tissue paper from the effect of the stomach acids. It was torn during the surgery, but that was repaired. During the week of hospitalization, we were thankful for the competent doctors and nurses God had provided.

In the first few days after surgery, Matthew suffered complications, and infection set in. We alternated staying at motels near the hospital and driving home. Norm would go to the counseling center during the day and return to the hospital later. He gave me emotional support and understood that I needed to be there at Matthew's bedside.

Daily, I prayed on the phone with my best friend. After many years of praying with her, it was a comfortable, natural way to weather a crisis. We were also sustained by the prayers of Matthew's sister, his grandmothers and our other friends.

One beautiful morning, as I drove to the hospital, this Scripture came on the radio: "For I am convinced that neither death, nor life, nor angels, nor principalities, nor things present, nor things to come, nor powers, nor height, nor depth, nor any other created thing, shall be able to separate us from the love of God, which is in Christ Jesus our Lord" (Rom. 8:38-39, *NASB*). The phrase "death, nor life" seemed to stand out. I knew in my heart that Matthew's life was in the balance, and I marveled at the security we have in God's love.

Early on, the nurses seemed relieved that I was there, and they asked me questions since they couldn't communicate with Matthew. They let me know my presence was needed. I felt that being his mother was a special privilege. Their main question was, "How does he show he's in pain?" They needed to know when to give him medication. I was eager to help in any way I could, but I was at a loss to answer that question. (They had no choice but to just medicate him at regular intervals.)

As I visited each day, our time together was special. I patted Matthew's hand and talked to him in simple, loving words. He didn't reach out and respond, but his eyes followed me as I moved about the room. It was touching to see him content and peaceful, even during his times of discomfort.

I was aware of God's presence through the days at the hospital. I was reassured that He was in control, and I had a sense of being uplifted by the prayers of family and friends. I was even able to reach out to a family dealing with their son's tragic motorcycle accident, which had caused massive trauma to his head.

After a week, additional surgery was performed. Following the operation, Matthew stayed in the intensive care unit. He was heavily sedated and unconscious. There were eight tubes in him, and he was constantly on a ventilator. He developed adult respiratory disorder syndrome. We were hopeful when the fever dropped and his blood pressure stabilized, but in several days we could see that he was not responding. The doctors felt he was in the Lord's hands. We prayed at his bedside for the Lord's will to be done.

We had stayed at our home the night of March 14 instead of a motel near the Loma Linda Hospital. I woke up at

4:00 AM. with the feeling that Matthew was worse. I called the hospital, and the staff confirmed my fears. They had gone to full power on the ventilator. Around 7:00 AM. that morning, as we were getting ready for the day, we received a phone call. It was one of the medical staff, and he said, "You need to be here as soon as possible." His request didn't need any amplification.

Fortunately, we were able to speed through the traffic, those 60 miles to the hospital. Both of us were aware that it could be Matthew's final hour. We had not seen any response from him for days.

Norm and I walked into the room, and the doctors told us that Matthew's lungs and heart were failing and would probably stop in about an hour. My initial response, which might surprise you if you've never had a loved one suffer and die, was profound joy. I was truly happy for him. I said, "Oh, he'll be in the presence of the Lord this day!" I knew he would be finished with the struggles of this world, totally healed, and finally out of pain.

We both felt that way. But we also felt helpless since there was nothing anyone could do to make Matthew well again. As much as we knew he was going to a far better place, we also knew we were facing the greatest loss of our lives.

We said goodbye to Matthew, and I prayed at his bedside, thanking the Lord for our precious child and for His provision of eternal life. As we stood there, we saw Matthew's pulse rate decline ten beats. We felt as though we were giving him back to God and saying, "He's Yours. Have Your perfect will with him." We believed God had something better for him.

Matthew's decreasing vital signs confirmed the reality that he was going to die soon. The doctors said we could stay there or wait in the family room, and we chose the latter. Within an hour, the doctors came to tell us Matthew had died. We cried and talked with them. God was truly loving and merciful when He took Matthew home that day, and we bowed to His perfect will. Perhaps others won't understand our mixture of feelings, but that's all right. We felt peace.

I learned a lot about Norm from our son's death. It revealed to me his depth of emotion, love and caring. I was amazed at how tender his feelings were and how easily the tears came from him. We were more aware of our oneness as we shared our grief and discussed how the Lord had gently prepared us for this time. Tears also have been a friend to me. Often they will come during a worship experience, and I become aware of the Holy Spirit's comfort and healing in my heart. They also come at some of the most unexpected moments.

As we know so clearly, the death of a child is unlike any other loss. It's a horrendous shock, no matter how it happens.

One of the most difficult and disturbing issues is the wrongness of a child's death. It just shouldn't happen. It doesn't make sense. It's death out of turn. The parent often feels, *Why should I survive when my child, who should survive, didn't?* Death violates the cycle that children grow up and replace the old.

A mother summed up the experience:

The search for some meaning in a child's death is an ongoing rumination for survivors. It is as if we must unearth every detail surrounding the death, so we can begin to piece together this incomprehensible tragedy. When nothing makes sense, we desperately search for some small clue, some piece of evidence that will complete the puzzle.[1]

Years ago, when infectious diseases ran wild, child death was common. Today most deaths occur naturally and expectedly among the elderly. Our society is prepared for death with this group and handles it relatively well. The thought-to-be-infrequent occurrence of child death is more traumatic.

The death of a child is a parent's worst nightmare.

If you have lost a child, you may think you're the victim of an assault, and you are. Who you are—your identity—has been attacked. The more you have invested yourself in another's life, the more you have to lose; so the pain of your separation from your child is especially intense because of the closeness that is now gone.

There are other significant losses as well. Your family, as you have always known it, is forever changed and diminished by the loss. Your old family structure and system are gone, and you need to create new ones.

> When a child dies, the very ground on which we depend for stability heaves and quakes and the rightness and orderliness of our existence are destroyed. Nothing in life prepares us; no coping skills were learned. Parents who lose children are thrown into chaos.[2]

Secondary Losses

The loss of your child creates many secondary losses. As a parent, you have hopes, dreams and expectations for your children. These, too, have vanished, and you feel cheated. These losses will need to be grieved as well—an abundance of things your child will never do. The losses could include graduation, sports, the wedding or the birth of grandchildren. Author Catherine Sanders says it well:

> Our children are our tomorrow. From the moment of conception—even before—we fantasize about their futures, what they will become, what they will be like, who they will marry, how many children they will have. We see ourselves in the role of grandparents. And, why not? This is what we have learned to expect. This is the correct order of the universe. We count on it.
>
> It is no wonder, then, that when our children die and the chain of order is broken, we can't comprehend it. Our future has been blunted, perhaps even stolen, buried with our dead child.[3]

You struggle with the time in your life. It now takes on a new meaning.

Have you ever been asked the question, "Pardon me, do you have the time?" The question takes on new meaning when you've lost a child. Elizabeth Mehren, in her book *After the Darkest Hour,* poignantly describes the "before and after" aspect of a loved one's loss:

> Ask a person on the street—I almost said a "normal" person, because that is how we sometimes think of ourselves: we, who have lost our own children, as contrasted with "normal" people, the rest of the world—and you will get one kind of answer. Most likely you will get a glimpse at the wrist, and in this world of digital exactness, you will get the hour, the minute and maybe the second as well. "One forty-two and twenty seconds, August the twenty-first." This is what most people, normal people, mean when they talk about telling time.
>
> But when you lose a child, a giant tectonic shift takes place. If you think of it in terms of chronometry, it is as if all your inner clocks are at rest. Chronologically, your interior calendar is wiped clean, but for one key date. There's now a new kind of before and after in your life: There's before your child died, and there's after your child died.
>
> Since the rest of the world persists in following a more conventional timetable, most of us keep these dates to ourselves. But they're finely etched into our brains, the way we memorize other vital statistics, like Social Security numbers or wedding anniversaries. You could shake most of us awake in the middle of a deep sleep and we could tell you how many days, weeks, months, or years have passed.
>
> It's our own secret system of measurement, our own private way of telling time. And it's normal. Perfectly normal.[4]

I've experienced this. Often I've said, "It's been _____ years since Matthew died."

You're aware of your losses, but are you really? You can be so busy and overwhelmed that they accumulate and fester without your awareness of why you're feeling the way you do.

When you have the opportunity (or when you create it), make a list of your losses, for each one needs to be grieved. This is not a one-time event; losses continue to arise. Some of the losses I experienced with Matthew, who was developmentally disabled, were:

- I was the father of a son, but I didn't know what it meant to be the father of a son.
- Never being called "Daddy" or "Papa" or any term.
- Not having my family name continue.
- Not playing baseball with Matthew.
- Not taking him or teaching him to fish.
- Not experiencing all the normal developmental stages.
- Not having the "father and son talk."
- Not hearing him sing.
- Not seeing him accept the Lord and grow spiritually.
- Not being able to baptize him.

These are just a few of the losses.

What are your losses? Were you surprised by any? If you're married, what are your spouse's losses?

The Loss of Safety

Many of your values, your beliefs about life and God, have been assaulted as well. Most of us have beliefs and assumptions about our world. Many believe that the world is basically a good place and that most people are good, that most events and things turn out well. Many believe that we can make sense of the world and control the outcome of life events. Bad things happen to other people, not to good people, and not to us. Regardless of our beliefs and value systems, we tend to believe or at least live our lives as though they will not end; and we love those close to us as if they will not end. The phrase "You don't know what you have until it's gone" impacts most of us.

One author described our life in this way: "Many of us live privileged lives, taking for granted all that is cherished, all that is wonderful and all that is currently perfect in our lives. So we strive, compete, experience stress, overlook the fragility of our good fortune, and look ahead with anticipation—not dread."[5]

The death of a child destroys our life as though we live in a glass house and it just shattered. What we believed and knew has collapsed. What was stable has turned into a life of devastation. Not only is a child gone, but so is the life and assumption that we believed. Parents have said:

Our life changed with just a snap of the fingers. It hasn't, well, it's never been the same since.

Life just kind of fell apart. It really did.

It impacts every part of your life . . . and I realized fairly early on that things would never be normal again.

I think nature is very kind to you and provides you with this incredible numbness . . . it's like you're in a coma . . . you're here in a coma because it's nature's way of protecting you . . . it's quite amazing when you think about it. As the numbness starts to wear off and reality, it's like you have this coating of numbness and then that starts to dissolve and then you get this, the taste of the grief, the reality of what happened to you, you start to taste that. . . at about six months the realization hit, the numbness was gone.[6]

I've heard many parents say words to the effect, "My feeling and sense of safety have been taken away from me." It spreads to other areas of your life. There is a feeling of trepidation about the remaining children, and the world looks dangerous. Thoughts like these run through your mind:

I know I'm not here for a long time; it could happen tomorrow, it could happen on the way home.

We worry all the time [about the surviving child] . . . it's anxiety all the time, it's always there.

I'm more cautious about what's going on around me, realizing what the results of accidents are.

We could lose another child. It happened once, it could happen again. You thought nothing was ever going to happen to you, and when he died, you realized it can happen to you anytime, and it can happen again.[7]

You end up thinking, *If I was helpless in protecting this child, how can I expect to protect my other children?*

That feeling of an inability to protect your child spreads to anyone else who was involved in supposedly protecting your child. This could include emergency and ambulance staff, nurses, doctors, law enforcement personnel and even insurance representatives.

Your belief that others can protect your children has been shattered. You may experience both disappointment and anger toward those who were "supposed" to help.

The news of the death of your child is traumatic whether it was expected or sudden. Images may come back to haunt you, or you may develop avoidance fears related to where the loss occurred, or expect constant ambushes. Because of the trauma, for most people the intense emotions are too difficult to handle. Many feel overwhelmed and fragile. As one parent shared, "My life now is a constant battle—I feel like I'm fighting an unseen enemy."

One of the most traumatic types of loss of a child is by murder or manslaughter. A parent's mourning is more profound, lingering and complex than in normal grief. It was so sudden, violent and preventable, which creates a condition of complicated mourning for the loved ones.

Unfortunately, family members experience a double victim traumatization at this time. They are victimized by the criminal and what he or she has done and by the criminal system. Even if the person responsible has been caught, the time between apprehension, trial and prosecution stretches into months and years, which creates more trauma for the family. If the perpetrator is not caught and identified, the parents are denied the closure that is so important in dealing with the death of their child.

And then there is the presence and intrusion of the media. The potential for family and friends to feel victimized by police and other authorities only complicates the grieving process.[8]

The Loss of Future Plans
When you lose a child, you also lose what your child represented to you. You feel victimized in so many ways. You feel as though

you've lost part of yourself or even part of your physical body. Those features in the child that bore resemblance to you or your spouse hit the hardest.

You will miss the physical interaction—the sight, sound, smell and touch of your child. If you were still in the hands-on, caregiving stage with your child, this absence will be terribly painful.

Your child embodied your connection to the future, and that no longer exists. If your child was old enough to respond to you, you've lost a very special love source. That love was based on need, dependence, admiration and appreciation, but now it's gone. You've lost some of your own treasured qualities and talents as well, for you saw some of those that you value most in your child.

Further, you've lost the expectations and dreams you had for your child as he or she developed and grew older. Those anticipated years, full of so many special events, were ripped away from you.

An Altered View of Self

It's My Fault

You may also see your child's death as a failure on your part. You feel anger and frustration for being unable to exert some control over what happened to your child.[9]

Dr. Therese Rando graphically describes this feeling:

> With the death of your child you have failed in the basic function of parenthood: taking care of the children and the family. You are supposed to protect and provide for your child. You are supposed to keep her from all harm. She should be the one who grows up healthy to bury you.
>
> When you "fail" at this, when your child dies, you may feel that you have failed at your most basic function. . . .
>
> Disillusionment, emptiness and insecurity may follow, all of which stem from a diminished sense of self. And this can lead to the guilt which is such a common feature in parental grief.[10]

The "if onlys" plague many parents; I've heard so many of them. "If only I had gone to the beach with my husband. It's true he might have killed me, too, but maybe not. I could have kept him from killing Jimmy and Michael. I know I could have taken the bullets instead . . . if only I had been there . . . I should have done more . . ."

"If only I had given him money for gas, he wouldn't have gone on his skateboard. He was a good driver. I know he'd be alive today if I hadn't been so hard on him . . . I wish I could turn the clock back . . ."

"He left for work late that morning. If only I had woken him on time, he would have taken his regular bus and not the one his killer was on. I go over and over that in my mind. It shouldn't have happened. I could have prevented this if I had done my job . . ."

If onlys are a reflection of guilt—many parents feel they some-how caused their child's death or failed to protect their son or daughter or treated him or her badly, which caused the death. Some parents feel the death occurred because of their own prior behav-ior or some moral transgression, or they feel remorse over having survived the child. Guilt can surface over not feeling or expressing the appropriate emotions or grief, or when enjoyment enters their life again. This is the experience of recovery guilt. Do you identify with any of these?

When you grapple with guilt and self-blame, you end up en-gaging in *counterfactual thinking*. This is when you generate imag-ined or more positive alternatives to events that ended disastrously. The "what if" and "if only" statements (guilt producing) are exam-ples, and they often precede these counterfactual thoughts.[11]

It's not uncommon for parents to blame themselves for their child's death. Many carry on a court case in their minds. They're on trial, and they convict themselves and continually pronounce a verdict. The charges they pronounce against themselves are serious, and they themselves are a tough prosecutor.

I Am Unworthy

Parental guilt can take many forms. Some parents experience survi-vor guilt—the feeling that it's not right that they are still alive and their child isn't. There can also be illness-related guilt, where the parent thinks some personal deficiency caused the child's sickness and death. Some parents experience guilt over the belief that in some unknown way they either contributed to their child's death or failed to protect the child.

"I did the best I could" is usually concluded with, "but it wasn't enough." We end up believing that parental guilt is normal and justified. You don't have to have a good reason for guilt; it can be about anything. It doesn't matter how your child died; you feel guilty. Some of the guilt is tied to the fact that you're still alive and your child is not.

Those who lose a child to sudden death tend to feel more guilt than those who have anticipated their child's death. Those who seem to carry the heaviest load of guilt are those who lose their child to suicide.

Some experience moral guilt over the belief that the child's death was punishment for *their* violation of some moral or religious code.[12] As Dr. Rando explains:

> In those situations where the death results from genetic or unexplained medical factors, parents often take on additional burdens of grief. They try to explain why their child died prematurely and violated the laws of nature. Parents hold themselves responsible for not producing a healthy child that could survive longer, and often feel deficient and worthless as a result. Often, when answers about the cause of death are not forthcoming, parents tend to search all the way back to the earliest prenatal experiences in attempts to identify the reason for the medical condition: "Perhaps it was because I took the aspirin when I was pregnant that she developed the beginnings of the illness that took her life at 11."[13]

Because of all these losses, your grief over the death of a child will be more intense and last longer than grief over the loss of anyone else. The death of a child has been called the ultimate bereavement. You need to accept this and let others know about it as well.

I Feel Alienated

When parents lose a child, many feel as though they've been sent into exile. They're deported into a place they don't want to be. It's a land of experiences and difficulties that are unwanted, unfamiliar and painful. As one parent said, "We (bereaved parents) are *here*, but those who have not lost a child are *there*. They are alive but we are in the land of the dead."[14]

You feel disconnected from others, like you're in another world that others can't relate to. You feel different, even odd. It's not just that you feel different; others around you feel different as well. How does one talk with or interact with or help someone who is in exile? One set of authors describes it this way:

> For most parents, initial feelings of shock and disbelief, the most intense feelings of sadness and loss, the degree of loss of efficiency in daily living, and the experience of disconnectedness from other "non-exiles" decrease in intensity and frequency over time. However, it is also the case that for many parents, although typically occurring with less ferocity as time passes, the sense of yearning and sadness at a great loss will never quite go away. To paraphrase the ancient Hebrew prophet Jeremiah, Rachel cannot be comforted, because her children are no more.[15]

And the pain . . . it's overwhelming.

With reality comes pain, and the pain, when it comes, is stunning. The pain is actually physical, mostly in your stomach and chest. Your chest feels crushed and you can't seem to catch your breath. I remember feeling pinned like a butterfly, or somehow eviscerated. One woman drew an arc that started at her head and ended at her knees and said, "His death was cut out of *here*." The pain comes in waves, moves in, backs off, then in again. People try describing it with superlatives or metaphors, then give up the attempt. And no one wants to try too hard anyway; they'd much rather talk about how, with time, the waves of pain gradually become less frequent. "Now when I think of him," one woman said, "I don't get that *wrenching*, I don't know the word to use, that *wrenching* feeling."[16]

Will it last forever? Ann Finkbinder describes the pain in her book *After the Death of a Child*:

I don't think you're *ever* going to get over it. You make yourself go on with your life and do what you have to do, and you *are* happy. But you're not ever going to get over it. You'll never be *as* happy. You talk about getting better and the pain going away. I don't think the pain will go away until you die. When you take your last breath—then, it's gone.

There always is a void, a pain and a void that will never be filled again in your life. Even when life right now is going well, it's never fully total, complete happiness like there once was.

Very much in the beginning I felt completely dead inside. Now I don't feel completely dead, but I feel there's a part of me that is *gone*. That's a cross you bear. A weight in your heart, a heaviness. An underlying sadness that's *there*.

You're scarred forever. I don't like it, I hate it. I feel like every morning I get up with this extra fifty pounds tied to my heart and I have to carry it.[17]

You'll continually struggle with anger—anger at what happened, at anyone you feel could have prevented it, at the unfairness of what transpired, at the disruption of your life, and at God. The anger will come and go for years.

Do you relate to these statements? Does this describe your journey? For many it does.

As a bereaved parent, you'll have to "grow up with the loss." Parents tend to mark their lives by the events and accomplishments that would have involved their children. The dates when those events would have occurred will still come around, even though your child won't be there to experience them. The sixth birthday; the first teen birthday; the times when your child would have received a driver's license, graduated, married and had children; all will bring a resurgence of your grief when you least expect it.

Loss by Terminal Illness

When your child dies because of a terminal disease, you get a double dose of grief. Before your child's death, you grieve over the fact that your child is going to die. Afterward, you grieve the actual death.

Even though you know it's going to occur, and you've known that for weeks, months or years, it's still devastating.

The trauma of coping with a terminally ill child redefines your entire life. Perhaps you've never experienced this trauma yourself, but we are called to be compassionate and supportive of others. Knowing what other parents face may speak to your heart. When a child is dying, it's as though the future is canceled for a time. The entire focus is on the present. Priorities change and future plans and dreams are jeopardized. If the future is considered at all, it's thought of with dread. Read the words of fathers and mothers who have lost a child after a long illness:

> A mother whose 17-year-old son died of bone cancer: "There was no future for us. We were afraid of what to-morrow and the next day might bring. We learned to sa-vor every good moment, every good day. We didn't allow ourselves to even think beyond that day. The future was a frightening place for us."

> A father whose four-year-old son died of leukemia: "We had to readjust our whole life when Sam became ill. All our future plans had to be shelved. I didn't even want to think about the future because I knew it held Sam's death. It was just too unbearable to think about."

> A mother whose six-year-old daughter died of leukemia: "Her death was not imminent to me. This was something in the future; it was far away. I lived only for today. I didn't even think about tomorrow, let alone plan for it."[18]

When your child is diagnosed as terminal, it may take days for reality to sink in.

If you were the parent of a terminally ill child, you probably ex-perienced one or more of the following common reactions: You may not have accepted the diagnosis and prognosis when initially re-vealed to you. (This also happens when you're told your child has a disability.) You assimilate this kind of information gradually or deny it right up to the last moments you have with your child.

Perhaps you fantasized consciously or subconsciously about a miraculous recovery for your child.

You may have arranged a healing service, asking the elders of the church to anoint your child with oil and pray. You may have provided a special diet; sought a special treatment banned in this country; used visualization techniques; or bargained with God.

You may have felt that your child's illness was some sort of punishment for something you did in the past or even thought about.[19]

No matter how a parent loses a child, the questions arise: "How do I recover? What steps can I take to survive?"

Life in the Weeks and Months After Loss

We've looked at loss and grief in an overall manner, but let's consider other aspects now.

Although your child has died, he stays intensely alive in your mind. Part of what makes grieving such a long and painful haul is this jarring discordance. In your mind he is a vital presence, and you love him more than ever. Yet every day a hundred things remind you that he is not here. How to make sense of these two? How can you possibly sweep up the heart and put love away?

From your experience of other losses, you know that the person you loved stays forever with you but slowly recedes from center stage. As time passes, you find ways to hold on to what you loved best about the person, notice the ways in which he has become a part of you. As these shifts occur, you gradually recover your capacity to invest in relationships, to allow another person onto center stage.

The way your child stays with you, woven through your thoughts and your imaginings, marks the loss of a child as different from any other loss.

You will find ways to keep your child. You will find ways to keep the parts of you that have wrapped themselves around her. You will sense her presence, find her in your dreams, talk to her. Slowly, as you are ready to have it happen, you will move her from center stage. But she will never be unseen. You will have her for all of your life.[20]

The Physicality of Grief Recovery

Fatigue is one response, but with the death of a child, parents talk more about feeling depleted, drained. They feel empty. You may feel constantly tired, and nothing seems to alleviate the problem; everything seems to be too much to do. There's a drain on what energy you have, and if you go back to work, you feel like you have to keep pushing and pushing. Many feel as if they've aged 10 years overnight. It's like you've developed an immunity to rest, for it doesn't seem to do any good.

Everyone responds differently. Some immerse themselves in minutia, trying to feel every moment, while others become inactive and helpless. Some sit and stare and fail to eat or take care of their personal hygiene. They have a zombie-like appearance, and this can last for weeks or months. It usually subsides gradually. They tend to be numb rather than in pain. Both pain and positive feelings are deadened. One parent described this condition so accurately: "The ability to feel pleasure takes a long time to return. All activity takes on a robot-like quality. Life goes on by rote."[21]

The Practical Issues of Remembering Your Loved One

You're faced with many practical questions: What do you do with your child's room and belongings? What will you decide to keep that reminds you of who your child was? Will your child's room be used and just "be there"? How soon do these decisions need to be made?

There is no best way to decide. Each parent and each family responds differently. Each person needs the opportunity to express their wishes in terms of timing and what to do with the belongings. And some may want to wait, while others want to respond now.[22]

A parent dealing with his or her child's empty room might describe the experience this way:

We wanted to move, but if we do, then we have to empty Jimmy's room. We've kept it intact since he died, and we go in there now and then and sit on the bed and cry. But what will we do if we move? We won't have room for all of his things. I'm, we're not ready to say goodbye to his stuff. Putting his things away is another loss. It's like denying who he was and is, and it's like we're closing the door on him if we do this. I don't want him gone. Isn't there some way to have some kind of a new relationship with him? I still want him here in some ways.

Barbara Rosof describes the spectrum of responses parents may display as they deal with the practical, day-to-day reminders of their child's absence:

Feelings get lodged in the details and the daily routines of our lives. You can talk about large, abstract topics such as loss and parenting and grieving, and not feel a thing. But talk about when you were folding a load of clothes, and there were your son's jeans, and your feelings well up.

Sorting through your child's possessions is the kind of practical task that brings up feelings, requires you to think about what has happened. Folding his jeans, stacking his tapes, you are reminded again and again of what will never be. In the face of these hands-on reminders, the most tenacious denial gives way.[23]

As a parent, and especially as a mother, some sort of bond or connection will continue. Your child is still an important part of your life and will be forever. Bedrooms may remain as they were; or if not, there will be shelves with items and pictures as well as references to who he or she was or what he or she did.

Parents say:

She's here with me in some way all the time.

I'll always have her in my life. I think of how old she would be, but remember who she was then.

We still write letters each year and leave them at the gravesite. I tell him what he's missed and how we miss him.

I see him every day in the tree we planted in the backyard. It's a reminder, not just a memorial.

Many talk about keeping their child present in some way, and each family has to find what works best for them. What remains are memories, your child's influence, what he or she meant to you, what he or she taught you and influenced you. Your child, no matter what age, left you a legacy. My son, Matthew, through his life, changed me from a non-expressive, not-in-touch-with-my feelings, non-crying man into just the opposite, because of who he was years before his death. With his expressive eyes he taught me to listen since he had so few words and couldn't communicate normally.

For a long time after your loss, you will live in a dark tunnel, not sure there's any light at the end. But when you keep searching for it, you will find it. This grief lingers longer than any other, and you will carry the remnants of shadow grief for years.

Ronald Knapp, in his book *Beyond Endurance—When a Child Dies*, gives us an insightful description of shadow grief:

Shadow grief reveals itself more in the form of an emotional "dullness," where the person is unable to respond fully and completely to outer stimulation and where normal activity is moderately inhibited. It is characterized as a dull ache in the background of one's feelings that remains fairly constant and that, under certain circumstances and on certain occasions, comes bubbling to the surface, sometimes in the form of tears, sometimes not, but always accompanied by a feeling of sadness and a mild sense of anxiety. Shadow grief will vary in intensity depending on the person and the unique factors involved. It is more emotional for some than for others.

Where shadow grief exists, the individual can never remember the events surrounding the loss without feeling some kind of emotional reaction, regardless of how mild.

The difference between "normal" grief and "shadow" grief is similar to the difference between pneumonia and the common cold. The latter is less serious, less disruptive to life, more of a nuisance than anything else.[24]

The Unpredictability of Emotions

Grief has a beginning, middle and end, but no one can tell you how long this grief will last. Many parents get stuck in the middle, and most don't understand the dynamics and duration of grief, which makes it even more difficult to adjust.

Your tears will come for years. Let them. One morning, tears hit me in our worship service at Hollywood Presbyterian Church. The service focused on Pentecost. As the organ played, the sound of a brass quartet suddenly filled the air. Trumpets always brought a response from Matthew. He would look up with an alertness or wonderment in his expression, as if to say, "Oh, that's something new."

The sound of the brass in the service brought back another memory: Matthew's joyful laughter. Years ago, I decided to take up the trumpet (which lasted only a few years). I purchased a horn and took weekly lessons. During one of Matthew's visits home, I began to practice. He looked at me with an expression that said, "I don't believe what I'm hearing!" He listened to another squawk, threw back his head and laughed harder than we had ever heard him laugh. Again and again, he laughed and giggled until we were all in stitches. My novice attempts to play had at least pleased him. Needless to say, these memories brought the tears once again.

Another time, I was driving home and listening to Chuck Swindoll's radio program. During the message, he listed the names of Jesus' disciples. Hearing him say the name Matthew brought my sense of loss and sadness to the surface, where it stayed for several days. Who would have thought that would cause such a reaction?

Then there were times when my feelings were just flat. A low-grade numbness set in, and I wondered when the pain would hit again. Just three months after Matthew died, I had been very busy with work and projects. For several days, there had been little feelings and no tears. As I told a client what had happened, however, the tears came to my eyes. Then as I sat with the parents of a profoundly disabled child, trying to help them, the tears again rose to the surface. Next, I received a note from a friend who had lost his 19-year-old son in an accident more than four years earlier. When he said the pain was sometimes as fresh as if it had just happened, I wondered, *Will it be that way for us?* Again my tears clouded over.

During that dry time, as I refer to it, grief hit hard once more. I was riding my exercise bike and listening to a worship tape by Terry Clark. One of the songs was "I Remember." As I rode, I was also working on a new catalog to send to people who had attended our seminars over the years. I was wondering whether to include anything about Matthew, since most of the people had heard our story. I had considered saying, "For years we had prayed for Matthew to be whole. On March 15, God saw fit to make him whole."

As I thought about that (and perhaps because of the music and the fact that I was planning to visit his grave for the first time), the flood occurred. The sense of loss was overwhelming, and I wept intensely. One thing I've learned: you never apologize for your tears.[25]

As I was writing this chapter and looking once again at some of the notes we received and my written thoughts, the feelings and tears rose once more to the surface. I found two written responses to my tears that I had put in a folder. This first one I wrote nine months after Matthew's death:

January 5, 1991

Where have the tears gone? There was a time when I thought they would never end, but now I miss them as though they were a friend. There's only a mist where once a stream, the memories are fading all too fast, like it was last night's dream. It seems too soon to be this way, but I realize they may return yet another day. Who would have thought the sobs and clouded eyes would be missed, but they are. And yet, even as this is written, the words are difficult to see for some strange reason.

The poems and letters from friends help to bring back the loss again. Words of comfort expressed at the time of deepest pain help to keep Matthew's memory alive. For that's all we have of him now are memories. Someone else has the joy of his presence, his laugh, his smile, and his hugs.

Where have they gone? They haven't. They were hiding and waiting once again for the time to be called out and express the loss. They're here again, not as an intruder, but as a welcomed friend. Please don't stay away so long the next time. I need you. We need you.

Then in the fifteenth month, I wrote:

It's been some time since the feelings came to the surface. You begin to wonder if they ever will again. But then they do. And each time is different. It began with finding some old pictures of Matthew when he was quite young, and in most of them he was smiling. Two days later we were watching Dr. Ogilvie on a Sunday morning TV program, and he read the passage in which the centurion came to Jesus about his son who was dying. Jesus told him to go home, his son would live. Both Joyce and I had the same response, "I wish that Jesus would have made that statement to us about Matthew." The tears came that morning. They will always be there and come when you least expect them. But they were there as part of our connection with something that we valued but lost, at least for the present time. They are also a reminder that our life is a series of transitions and changes, some of which we like and others we resist.

You can recover. It will take an understanding of the grief process, a change of attitude from thinking, *It will never end,* to thinking, *I will adjust and survive,* and a willingness to make the painful journey through the wilderness of grief.

Recovery Doesn't Diminish Memory

Most parents want to discover how to cope with their loss. Coping is tied to mourning. *Coping* means "struggling or contending with some success." An older meaning was to "strike back or fight." Mourning is all about actively and willingly working through your grief—striking or fighting back. It's the process of purging yourself of the grief over your loss.[26]

Ann Kaiser Stearns wrote, "All of us feel powerless at times because we are human beings. Triumphant survivors, however, trade in the position of helplessness for a decision to take charge and search for options."[27]

A unique factor is involved in the loss of a child. It's perhaps best summarized by the phrase "to never forget." Ronald Knapp describes it:

One important commonality that appeared to be character-istic of all parents who have suffered the loss of a child for whatever reason took the form of a need or desire; a need that makes the loss of a child different from other kinds of losses, and one that truly complicates the normal process of grieving. This is the need or desire never to forget—or to remember always!

The child is gone! Out of sight! And parents, mothers particularly, harbor a great fear that what memories they have of the child may eventually fade away. They fear that they will forget the sight of the child's face, the sound of his or her voice, the texture of the child's hair, the unique-ness of the hands, even the child's characteristic smell. Parents severely miss these sensual experiences and even-tually come to wish to retain them in memory for as long as they live.[28]

Reconnecting with Others

As you grieve, keep in mind certain steps that may be helpful. We've already talked about guilt, but a major task is to break that connec-tion. The longer you let it linger, the more it gains a foothold and takes up permanent residence. Self-blame will cripple you and your other family relationships. It may be guilt over something you did, something you didn't do, something you thought, or something you wished.

If others around you don't talk about the death or seem to avoid you or the subject, you may feel even more guilt, as though you did something wrong. But people avoid the subject for reasons that have nothing to do with blaming you. Most don't know what to say, and many feel anxiety over your child's death. They feel threatened. As a bereaved parent, you represent their worst fears; if it happened to your child, it could happen to theirs.

Unfortunately, such a seemingly callous response leaves you without support and fails to provide the validation you need about what has happened. Nothing hurts more than being ignored.[29]

Many parents feel their relationship with other people has changed. They're not as close. A distance has developed, which is related to the death of their child. Why? It's the word "nobody": "Nobody else understands"; "Nobody believes this can happen"; "Nobody knows the depth of pain." I hear this all the time—"Nobody gets it" is the phrase. You live in one world, and those who haven't lost a child live in another.[30]

Sometimes you just prefer to be alone and isolated. It takes energy that you don't have to be around other people and be where they expect you to be; you learn either to be an actor or to disappoint others.

One situation you may experience is the Christmas card effect. Often after a death you will receive cards and greetings from others who have no knowledge of your child's death. This may trigger various responses on your part. You may struggle with how to respond. Do you contact them immediately or wait until the season is passed? It may be better to wait but then let them know even if the death is several months ago. You could respond with, "I received your greetings and thank you. I'm sorry to have to tell you that (name) died on (date). I had hoped to contact everyone, but unfortunately missed a number. Please continue to pray for us." The situation is not limited to Christmas greetings, but with those you meet in the store, or phone calls.[31]

You may have to take the initiative to break the silence. When you talk about your child and what you've experienced, you let others know it's acceptable to discuss the death. If you feel you're being avoided, go to others and start conversations. Use a letter to help people know what you've experienced and how they can respond to you. That makes it easier to bring up the subject.

In a loving, gentle way, you need to let others know you will not be ignored. Then you will receive more care and support. Many are concerned that talking about your loss will intensify your pain. In some of the caring cards we received, we read statements like, "I hope this letter or card hasn't increased your hurt." But even if it did bring our pain to the surface, the comfort and connection from the card were worth it all.

5

Recovering from the Death of a Child

The loss of a child is one of the most painful journeys of life. To accomplish this journey, you need the help of others.

What are your sources of support? Even if you feel like withdrawing from everything and everyone, don't do it. Find your support. Identify that person or persons and a support group. Start making a list of the person or persons who will stand by you; and continue to reach out to them and stay connected. A support person needs to be accessible and available to you, experienced with a loss similar to yours, able to help you go on with your life and to help with tasks and errands you're unable to do during the grieving period.[1] (For support group information, see the appendix.)

We've already talked about survivor guilt. But there is something else that kicks in when you struggle with guilt: You're likely to concentrate on how perfect or good your child was. You tend to exalt all your child's positive traits, to idealize him or her. You think of your child as the "best" or the "most special."

If that happens, you're focusing on your deceased child to the detriment of your other relationships, and you're giving increased attention to what you're missing and longing for rather than on what you still have. If you have other children, you may be comparing them unfavorably to the child who died. They will make mistakes and may drive you up the wall. Deceased children don't

do that. They're saints frozen in time. This is somewhat normal
for a while, but in time, you'll be able to recall both the positive
and the negative experiences and balance will return.[2]

As you work through recovery, you may discover you have developed a new attitude toward death and your own dying. Studies
show that parents who have lost a child tend to no longer view death
as their enemy. Many find that it could be a friend, especially those
whose child went through a painful, lingering illness. For them,
death became a release and a relief. And as they dealt with their
child's death, they were able to handle the deaths of others more
effectively. Isn't it interesting that it often takes this experience to
make the truth of God's Word become a reality?

When you lose a child, there will be a time when your feelings of
separation and loss intensify and seem overwhelming. Your feeling
of being out of control is intense. The separation between you and
your lost child is more than you can handle. Some have an intellec-
tual awareness of the loss, but their emotions may not have caught
up yet. Some feel like they can barely hold it together emotionally.

If this sounds familiar to you, it's important not to run from
what you're experiencing, but to face the pain. Stuffing what you're
experiencing prolongs your agony.

What can you do to face the pain?

Never stop talking and sharing about your child. He or she is
on your mind, so give voice to what is there. Don't be concerned
about what others may be thinking. You won't really know anyway.
It's your grief and your thoughts and feelings.

As Harriet Sarnoff Schiff wrote in her well-received book *The
Bereaved Parent*, "The most essential ingredient . . . is surviving
well—besides facing reality—is to speak of the dead child unasham-
edly." For bereaved spouses and bereaved families, I encourage open
conversation about the child, about the spouses' own thoughts and
emotions, including shame and anger, but most especially about
their fears. We become frighteningly insecure in grief and we fear
that everything we know and love will be swept away, even ourselves. Only in hearing ourselves voice these thoughts out loud can
we finally begin to free ourselves from the dark elements of grief.[3]

Speak your child's name out loud. Let others know you want
them to talk about your child and call him or her by name.

Cry—it's natural, and you don't need to apologize. You need to cry, and so do those around you. Your crying gives others permission to do the same.

Anger will come—sometimes it's constant, and other times it comes and goes. It may be appropriate or it may be an overreaction to your situation. It may not make sense, and it doesn't have to. It needs an appropriate and healthy outlet, and that's where writing or journaling has been so beneficial. This outlet can keep us from being dominated by our anger.

No matter what you did, what you learned about parenting or how consistent you were in working toward being the best parent possible, guilt and shame will weave their way into your life.

You can expect to feel stressed. Your body has been called upon to respond in ways probably never experienced before. Your intense emotions demand energy, and extra adrenaline is being used to balance your emotions. You need to take care of yourself.

Don't be surprised by the amount of fear and anxiety you may experience at this time. Your fears will probably include personal concerns as well as for each of the other family members.

Overreactions may become a part of your life. This is not a lasting response; it is grief talking to you. There is a response we call "grief paranoia," which usually comes from the fear of feeling unsafe. There is no basis for this, but the smallest fear can become ingrained and continue to grow. Slights from others are magnified, and relationships may become strained.

Here are some Scripture verses that will be helpful at this time:

For God did not give us a spirit of timidity, but a spirit of power, of love and of self-discipline (2 Tim. 1:7).

So do not fear, for I am with you; do not be dismayed, for I am your God. I will strengthen you and help you; I will uphold you with my righteous right hand (Isa. 41:10).

But now, this is what the LORD says—he who created you, O Jacob, he who formed you, O Israel: "Fear not, for I have redeemed you; I have summoned you by name; you are mine" (Isa. 43:1).

> Do not be anxious about anything, but in everything, by prayer and petition, with thanksgiving, present your requests to God (Phil. 4:6).

Even though it may take an effort to show appreciation to those who are your true support, if they say they are praying for you, ask them how you could pray for them.[4]

If You Are a Stepparent

Families today are often blended families. You may not be the parent of the child who died, but what if you are a stepparent? A wide range of reactions could occur. For example, how close were you to this child, and how long was he or she in your life? How similar is your expression of grief to that of the biological parent? When there is a difference between the two of you, it's as though you have become strangers in some ways. It could be that others aren't aware of the depth of your relationship with this stepchild.

Sometimes a stepparent may have a feeling of relief for a multitude of reasons. One of the pressures a stepparent may experience is not being able to express true feelings to his or her partner. A stepparent cannot be expected to have the same closeness to the child as the biological parent. The child may have been in the home only part of the time, or the child and stepparent just didn't relate well to each other.

The child's birth parents may be drawn together at the dying and death of their child, perhaps even feeling that their child might still be alive if the marriage had survived. Either of the birth parents may feel responsible for the death of their child, or that the other was to blame, and there may be feelings of anger, guilt, remorse and failure. These emotions may last for months or years. There may also be practical difficulties to resolve, such as the wording on the headstone to reflect recognition and acceptance of both the birth parents and the stepparents' deep feelings toward the child.

A factor affecting stepparent grief may be the issue of who was physically caring for the child at the time of death. Anger and guilt are typical grief reactions but can be heightened when a stepparent is the caregiving parent when the death occurred.

A stepparent may feel almost invisible to the spouse, to other stepchildren, extended family, friends, clergy or medical personnel. Stepparents may find themselves excluded from important discussions about medical decisions or funeral arrangements. The assumption appears to be that the stepparent, unlike the biological parent, cannot possibly understand or feel the depth of the loss. Additional pain is felt when others, with no malice intended, fail to acknowledge stepparents or make insensitive remarks. Sympathy cards may not include a stepparent's name. All these things serve to remind stepparents that their pain and concern are often unrecognized, are seen as illegitimate or, at best, are misunderstood.

Be alert to the possibility that old unresolved emotional issues between the biological parents may become more pronounced after the death, especially if there had been conflicts over the parenting process. On the other hand, the biological parents may have a need at this time to cling together as they struggle with the loss, thus making a stepparent feel further isolated and even threatened. This is usually a temporary situation, but one that requires tolerance, restraint and understanding.

If you are a single parent, you will experience the loss just like anyone else. But there are some unique factors as well.

If You Are a Single Parent

What can you expect as a single parent? A single parent with children is usually a mother. Many times, a single parent is less likely to have support from others, and the child's father may or may not be in the picture to give emotional support. Whenever the child's father is not available, it places an extra burden on your shoulders. It may be more difficult to find someone with whom to share your feelings and pain about your child's death.

Here are some thoughts that may come to mind for the single parent:

- *How is my child's father coping? Does he even care? Does he hurt the way I do? What about his parents?*

- *Should I contact my child's father?* Use caution about calling him if there is a possibility of rejection. It is important to protect and take care of yourself during this time.
- When living with others—a roommate, your parents or other family members—will you be able to find the needed privacy to grieve?
- Feeling alone in your grief is normal, because only you can experience your pain. It is a lonely process, even when surrounded by others.
- Plan ahead for special days and holidays—mother's/father's day, the child's birthday, death date, Christmas and special events. Decide ahead of time how you would like to spend those days and what will make them meaningful for you.[5]

As you proceed through your valley of recovery, try these three suggestions that have meant the most to me: First, *pray*. Write out your prayers as you may sometimes write out your feelings in a journal. Don't edit your prayers; let your feelings flow. Second, *worship*—at home and in church, as though you're the only person there. Don't worry about what others might think of your feelings and tears. Third, *read Scripture*. Let the comfort of God's Word meet your needs. Read comforting passages again and again, to yourself and aloud.

God's words, read or spoken to us in time of need, give us the ability to survive. Here is a brief collection of promises for those who mourn:

> In all their distress he too was distressed, and the angel of his presence saved them. In his love and mercy he redeemed them; he lifted them up and carried them all the days of old (Isa. 63:9).

> The LORD is my shepherd (Ps. 23:1).

> For God so loved the world that he gave his one and only Son, that whoever believes in him shall not perish but have eternal life (John 3:16).

I am the resurrection and the life. He who believes in me will live, even though he dies; and whoever lives and believes in me will never die (John 11:25-26).

God will wipe away every tear from their eyes (Rev. 7:17).

He who goes out weeping, carrying seed to sow, will return with songs of joy, carrying sheaves with him (Ps. 126:6)

Come to me, all you who are weary and burdened, and I will give you rest (Matt. 11:28).

Praise be to God and Father of our Lord Jesus Christ, the Father of compassion and the God of all comfort, who comforts us in all our troubles (2 Cor. 1:3-4).

When you pass through the waters, I will be with you; and when you pass through the rivers, they will not sweep over you. When you walk through the fire, you will not be burned; the flames will not set you ablaze (Isa. 43:2).

The Spirit helps us in our weakness. We do not know what we ought to pray for, but the Spirit himself intercedes for us with groans that words cannot express (Rom. 8:26).

For I am convinced that neither death nor life, neither angels nor demons, neither the present nor the future, nor any powers, neither height nor depth, nor anything else in all creation, will be able to separate us from the love of God that is in Christ Jesus our Lord (Rom. 8:38-39).

My grace is sufficient for you, for my power is made perfect in weakness (2 Cor. 12:9).

Where Is My Loved One Now?

Ask all the questions you need to ask, and ask them again and again.

Often parents and others ask, "Where do children go when they die?" I believe the Scriptures tell us they go to heaven, into the presence of God. King David had an infant son who died when he was only seven days old. David's response indicates he believed his son went to a place where he, too, would go one day (see 2 Sam. 12:23). And that somewhere is *heaven*.

When anyone dies, the soul leaves the body. Our bodies are simply "tents" that house our spirits. Paul said that when we're away from the body, we're at home with the Lord (see 2 Cor. 5:8). He also seemed to indicate that when Christians die, they awake in glory (see 1 Thess. 4:14).

One of the books you may want to read at this time is *Safe in the Arms of God* by John MacArthur. This is one of the best books written for parents who have lost a child. Grieving parents will find answers to questions they have about where their child is now and if they will see their child again, and many more helpful answers to their questions.

Be patient with your recovery, but believe that you will recover. David Wiersbe offers good advice about believing:

> In grief God seems to have abandoned us. He hasn't. In grief we feel as if nothing matters. It does. Sometimes we think life is not worth living; it is! In times of sorrow people of faith have to "believe against the grain." In our weakness, God reveals his strength, and we do more than we thought possible.
>
> Faith means clinging to God in spite of circumstances. It means following him when we cannot see, being faithful to him when we don't feel like it.
>
> Mourners need a creed; it is "I believe!" we need to affirm this creed daily:
>
> • I believe God's promises are true.
> • I believe heaven is real.
> • I believe I will see my child again.

- I believe God will see me through.
- I believe nothing can separate me from God's love.
- I believe God has work for me to do.

"Believing against the grain" means having a survivalist attitude. Bereaved parents are survivors; they have endured.... Not only do they survive, but also out of grief they create something good.[6]

In time, as other parents have, you will find meaning in what you've experienced. Listen to the words of these parents:

I really don't know why this happened to us, but I've stopped looking for the answer! I just have to put my faith in the Lord's hands. . . . Only He knows—only He has the answers!

The Lord works in many strange ways. At first I simply could not fathom this, but then I accepted the Lord. . . . He must have had His reasons. Whatever they are, they are good enough for me.

At first I was confused and bewildered and angry. Why did this happen to us? Why did God permit this to happen? . . . Then I began to realize that it was the will of God. . . . Who am I to question further?

Nothing pacified me after Tommy's death. I couldn't understand how a loving God could allow such a thing. . . . However, I eventually came to realize that God was my greatest salvation, whatever His reasons are for taking Tommy, I can now accept them! I think of Him as holding Tommy in His arms until the day I can join him.

"The Lord giveth and the Lord taketh away"—that is a quote from the Bible! I never knew exactly what it meant until this thing happened. . . . You're right, I questioned! I was angry and filled with hate over the loss of our son . . .

However, the anger and hate softened as I accepted the
Lord. I put myself in His hands and immediately felt a
sense of peace overtake me.[7]

In an earlier chapter, I talked about saying goodbye to my
son, Matthew. We have said goodbye to him many times now,
in various ways, such as visiting his gravesite. For a young child,
there are many other ways to say goodbye, such as redecorating
a child's room or finally giving away his clothes. I've read some
goodbye letters to a loved one who has died. But when a young
child dies, I believe there's a difference.

When a Christian or a young child dies, he or she is able to
say hello to the Lord. This is why our feelings can sometimes be
a mixture of sadness and joy—we are saddened by our loss, but
there's also a sense of joy for what the deceased person is now
experiencing. We've felt this. We have a void in our lives, but
Matthew's life is now full and complete. The Christian death
is a transition, a tunnel leading from this world into the next.

Through Matthew's death, we learned, in a new way, about
the grace of God. It came from the responses of friends, people
we knew and others we hadn't met. We learned about the value
of their words, their silent presence and their phone calls that
continued not just for a few weeks but for years. We weren't
forgotten; nor was Matthew. When I talked about the impact of
his life on us as individuals and on our marriage, as I had done
for years, I had a new segment of his story to relate. And again,
we have seen how God has used that aspect of his life to minister
to others. It seems we now have a new ministry to parents who
have lost a child in death. That's how God takes the upsets in
life and gives them deeper significance.

Of the many responses we received after Matthew's death,
I would like to share two with you. A few days after the memorial service, I received a note in the mail with an original psalm.
It was written by one of my former seminary students who was
a professor in the department of Christian education at Talbot
Graduate School of Theology, where I was his professor. He said
he had "dabbled a bit in creative writing" and wanted to share
his concern with us.

This is what he sent, which we reprint with his permission.

A Psalm About the Loss of Treasure

Lord, you told us not to lay up for ourselves
treasure on earth.
You said moths and rust would corrupt
and thieves would break in and steal it.
You told us, Lord, to lay up our treasures in heaven.
You promised, Lord,
that moths and rust wouldn't corrupt those,
and You promised, Lord,
that thieves couldn't steal it either.

Well, that's what they did, Lord.
That's what my friends did.
My friends Norm and Joyce laid up their treasure in heaven.
Yes, they did.
That treasure which You had given them so many years ago now.
That treasure which they knew early
was not perfect.
That treasure which would need so much from them
but was no less treasure just the same.
They called the treasure Matthew, and they loved him;
oh, how they loved him!

In just a small collection of minutes they knew something
was seriously wrong.
Matthew was not like other Matthews, or Andrews,
or treasures by any other name.
Matthew was different, and they came to even
love the difference in their treasure.

Now, Lord, now . . . What about your promise?
You promised thieves wouldn't steal.
I, and my friends, believed your promise.
But their treasure is taken from them.
Isn't that stealing?

H. NORMAN WRIGHT

OK. You took the treasure.
And I, and my friends, don't really know why.
But, you did, and maybe one day I can say,
"That's OK."
But right now, I can't.
I wonder if my friends can say that.
I don't know, but if they can, they know you
better than I do, I guess.

But what of their treasure, Matthew?
Is he running and playing in your heaven today?
Can he speak and say things like
"ice cream" and "chocolate candy" and "going fishing"?
Things he could never say to Norm and Joyce?
Can he laugh and hug and squeal and say,
"I love you, Mom!"
Maybe my friends are really gonna like what
you've done with their treasure.
Maybe just "one world away"
they're gonna see their treasure again
and say, "Boy, that's great!"
Maybe they are beginning, even now, to understand
That Matthew is really *your* treasure.
I don't understand that exactly,
but maybe my friends do.

Help them, Lord!
Please be the things to them I wish I could be, but can't.
Maybe you can say to Joyce,
"I love you, Mom,"
and she'll understand.
Maybe you can say to Norm,
"Let's go fishing, Dad,"
and he'll know what that means.

Thank you, Lord, for understanding me
and for comforting my friends.
I love you—and I know they do too.[8]

A few days following Matthew's death, we held his service. It was inspiring, encouraging and comforting. Our pastor, Dr. Lloyd Ogilvie, of the Hollywood Presbyterian Church, took several minutes to read passages from God's Word, and it struck us anew how much comfort there is in simply hearing it.

He closed the service with the following words:

"And Jesus said except you become as a little child you cannot enter the kingdom of heaven." We meet together with the assurance that Matthew, though childlike in spirit, knew that relationship with Jesus Christ by Christ's election and love and acceptance that made his death but a transition into the midst of living. And as the fellowship of faith this afternoon, we claim that Paul has said, "Our bodies are sown in weakness but raised in power." That is now true for Matthew. Handicapped? I would said "handicapable," for most of the attributes that we develop in life keep us *from* rather than bring us to the Father. The simple trust that we knew as a child is often blighted by the growth of our theories, our supposed maturity. Over and over again every day of our lives, we must become a child again and run to our Father and know His love and His forgiveness.

You can just imagine that the company of heaven today has a new voice. It's Matthew's voice singing with the angels and archangels around the throne of God, whole, complete in Christ. A miracle? Oh yes. But God's miracle is offered to each of us this afternoon. If this were our day, could we run to our Father with that same kind of trust and know for sure that we were going to spend eternity with Him?

Oh, Matthew taught his family so much. And he continues teaching here today. But there's nothing we can do to achieve our righteousness with God. There's not one thing that we can say or accomplish or write or speak that will make God love us any more than He does right now. That's what Matthew taught and teaches by his life. So much of our time is spent trying to accomplish those things that we think will make God take notice of us. But He loves us just as we are, as He loved Matthew.

One of my favorite stories that I think of often is of that semaphore message that was sent about Wellington's battle at Waterloo. You remember. It was interrupted halfway through when the clouds came down over the English Channel. The semaphore worded it out, "Wellington defeated . . ." and then the fog came down and the rest of the message didn't reach England for 48 hours. When the fog lifted, the semaphore completed the message, "Wellington defeated the enemy."

Our faith in Christ is that Matthew defeated all of the enemies—the enemies of disabilities, of incompleteness, and death. And his voice now has not just eight to ten words but a thousand tongues to sing Christ's praise, and in that we rejoice. Hallelujah, hallelujah, hallelujah.

We so appreciated Dr. Ogilvie's sermon and his abundant use of Scripture for the strength they gave us. Following the message, a friend and classmate from Westmont, Paul Sandberg, concluded the service by singing "No More Night." The words of one portion of this song of hope and triumph are "No more night, no more pain, no more tears, never crying again. Praises to the great 'I AM,' we will live in the light of the risen Lamb."[9]

Hope will return. God's comfort is sufficient.

6

Loss Before and After Birth

Losing a child is always difficult—for all the reasons we've discussed. But parents who lose a child by stillbirth or in early infancy often face an even harder time, for the death of such a young child is usually not considered as serious by some as the loss of an older child. There seems to be a prevailing attitude that says, "In a child's death, the younger the child, the easier it is; the older the child, the harder it is."

In the past, society viewed survivors of miscarriage as illegitimate mourners. However, miscarriage is an overwhelming journey for parents, as described by this author:

> Perhaps the utter powerlessness implied by the loss of an unlived life is simply unacceptable. It may be too great a reminder that despite all the modern day medical miracles that have both extended the human life's span beyond what was thinkable even a few generations ago and virtually assured the survival of even the tiniest premature baby—despite all the control over life that we have gained—death is our common destiny. Perhaps this is the ultimate fact that we seek to avoid by our silence.[1]

Today, circumstances are much different. Families are changing. Choosing to have only one or two children, or having children at an older age, or raising children as a single parent make for smaller families. We also seem to have an increasing number of couples that are unable to have children of their own. This is a major loss that frequently isn't recognized, so encouragement and support are often lacking for those who are childless. Kim Luger-Bell speaks to often-unrecognized child loss in her book *Unspeakable Losses*:

> A heavy shroud of silence surrounds pregnancy losses of any kind. These are private, intensely personal affairs. There is often shame and a desire to forget, and, especially with the chosen loss of abortion, a fear of condemnation, of being blamed for a deep parental failure.
>
> It seems so hard to talk about. There is a hesitancy to say it out loud, to name the experience to own it.
>
> Perhaps part of the reason is that the losses of pregnancy seem so intangible and unreal, especially in the case of pregnancies that end before a heartbeat is heard, or an abdomen begins to swell. But even in the case of later pregnancy losses, such as second-trimester miscarriages, or stillbirths, there are no memories to hold on to, no life to recall outside of the womb, only fantasies of who these babies might have been.
>
> Perhaps the most invisible childbearing loss of all is the hidden grief of those who, after long delays in childbearing because of the lack of a suitable relationship or sufficient financial security, have been unable to have the children they wanted and always thought they would have.[2]

Loss by Infertility

Infertility. The very word strikes fear into the hearts of couples. It is another loss of a child—the child that will never be. My daughter and her husband went through this experience. It's painful. Debra Bridwell wrote a book with a letter that describes the experience. Her book *The Ache for a Child* is a good resource for those who grieve for the child who will never be.

Another woman described what this experience can be like:

In the six years following the birth of my son, I lost two ectopic pregnancies, requiring the removal of both fallopian tubes. I also experienced four IVF (in vitro fertilization) failures in which living embryos were transferred to my womb, but failed to implant. Like many others, I tried to distract myself from my sadness and pretend it wasn't there. My focus during those six long years was almost continually on trying to have another baby, and not on the babies I had lost. When the inevitable feelings of helplessness, anger and envy arose, I condemned myself for being overly dramatic.

It is a fairly typical strategy for coping with these losses to keep the door shut tightly against one's sorrow. And as a result, the grieving process is often long and hard and slow. The tears I rejected came only when I slept. For six years I woke myself sobbing for those babies only in my dreams.

However, infertility is a loss that leads to what many professionals refer to as *hidden grief*. It doesn't get expressed publicly. That's because the loss brought about by infertility is not as widely understood as the loss experienced when a loved one dies. Infertility is intangible, whereas death is tangible. Infertility cannot be touched or seen, so its bearers hide their sorrow, complicating their grief and prolonging their healing.[3]

The psalms record some fitting descriptions of these emotions:

Save me, O God. The floods have risen. Deeper and deeper I sink in the mire; the waters rise around me. I have wept until I am exhausted; my throat is dry and hoarse; my eyes are swollen with weeping, waiting for my God to act (Ps. 69:1-3, *TLB*).

When I am overwhelmed and desperate, and you alone know which way I ought to turn (Ps. 142:3, *TLB*).

The discovery that infertility describes your childbearing life is like discovering one of your limbs is paralyzed. Everything appears normal until it's time to use it. And the discovery creates some very normal and predictable responses, beginning with, "There must be some mistake! Not us." The shock and denial are valid and even necessary.

> When denial and disbelief are maintained long enough, they war on significant relationships. When one spouse is in denial but the other is not, intense conflict arises. One spouse may be ready to move on, to pray about options, to grieve, to mourn, but the other doesn't even acknowledge that anything is wrong. The longer this conflict goes on, the more division the couple will have. Pretty soon, they will have two issues to grieve—the loss of a dream and the loss of a relationship.
>
> There may also be division among close friends. It is more difficult to maintain denial when your closest friends are having babies. You may find yourself avoiding them as a way of avoiding the pain of childlessness that you are afraid of feeling. You may find yourself withdrawing, isolating yourself from friends who were once a source of strength and encouragement while inviting in other childless couples who don't interfere with your denial.[4]

Naturally, the next step is an investigative and exploratory mission: "Why?" "Why us?" "Why is this happening?" Then the frustration and anger emerge. It can be directed at everyone: doctors, nurses, a spouse, family members, those who can get pregnant, those who have abortions, and so on.

Unfortunately, many who are facing infertility begin the process of self-blame and feeling that they are defective. A person's sense of value and worth can be quickly eroded and can lead to not wanting to be around others or able to handle others' responses. All the responses of grief that others who experience any kind of child loss will be present.[5]

It's been said that those who face infertility don't experience what is called a "clean grief," because infertility is an ongoing loss that comes and goes every month. Every 30 days there is hope and then disappointment and grief. For some, this pattern has lasted for years.

Grief over the child gets disrupted because of all the other ongoing losses. Consider what happens to your daily life—the loss of privacy; the loss of a sense of control; loss of purpose in life; loss of time, money, and time spent on building a career; the loss of having grandchildren in the future or providing your parents with grandchildren; of experiencing parenthood; of being needed; of being accepted by other parents. These and other losses lead many women to say this is the most upsetting experience of their life.[6] This loss encourages one to maintain hope, but consider this view:

> Uncertainty related to infertility keeps couples from moving ahead in the absence of a definite beginning and ending. Some have said that infertility is more like mourning someone missing in action than mourning someone known dead. After the bombing of the Oklahoma City federal building, a husband who had waited several days before receiving confirmation of his wife's death, said, "I actually feel relieved. Now I know for sure. Waiting and not knowing was the worst part."
>
> Sometimes hope becomes the enemy. Disappointment can be as hard to endure as other life crises. The more optimistic an infertility patient is at the beginning of the month, the harder the crash at the end. As Solomon said so well, "Hope deferred makes the heart sick" (Prov. 13:12).[7]

When a miscarriage occurs, as it does in as many as 25 percent of all pregnancies, a couple often receives little or no support. And whatever comfort is offered doesn't last long. In many cases, the expectant mother's pregnancy wasn't showing, so no one but her spouse assists her in the bereavement or shares in the memories.

The intensity of and amount of grief are tied not to the length of time the unborn child was carried, but to the hopes, values, needs, feelings and expectations the parents placed on that child. Parents begin to bond with their child before birth. They celebrate the news of pregnancy and usually share it quickly. They dream of the baby's first step, or a family Christmas, and often run through the child's life in their thoughts.

When the miscarriage occurs, the dreams die as well. You can imagine the intensity of the grief when a couple has been trying for a child for years, or the husband and wife are approaching age 40.

The grief can also be intensified if there is a continual string of miscarriages. Multiple miscarriages are a real possibility for many couples. In one study of 1,010 family members who had experienced a miscarriage, the mother averaged 1.9 miscarriages. One mother said she had experienced 15 miscarriages, only 1 child out of 16 pregnancies survived. Her marriage didn't make it.[8] Studies indicate that with miscarriage, the "average recovery time" is approximately 9 to 15 months.[9]

Following a miscarriage, too often what people say offers little comfort: "You're young; you can try again." "You're probably better off; something could have been wrong with the child anyway, and that would have been so hard." "In a sense it's good it happened to you since you're a strong person and can handle it. I never could."

If you've suffered a miscarriage, let others know about your grief. If it has happened to acquaintances, reach out and help them grieve.

Sometimes parents want to see the miscarried child, and sometimes they don't. Some parents are given Polaroid pictures of the ultrasound, tracing the child, if he or she was old enough. That can help to make the situation more real. Some parents name their child and have a service for him or her.

One couple I worked with knew at four months that their child had a rare condition and would not go full term. At six months, the little girl died, and the father told me how he took her outside and held her as he looked at the stars, prayed over her and committed her to the Lord.

If other people don't understand what you're doing, and they try to give you counter-advice, just remember that they usually are not experts and are speaking out of their own anxiety and dismay. You're free to grieve as much as you feel the need to. Be aware that there will be trigger points for your grief: the anniversary of when the child would have been born will hit you, and it could continue to hit you for years.[10]

Some people observe a childless woman and say to themselves, "She needs to stop baby craving." Yet would we expect a fueled fire to stop itself? Expect people to stop dying? Rainfall to sit on the surface of the earth? In general, God instilled in women the need to bear and nurture children. So the tears an infertile woman sheds simply validate the truth of what God said in Proverbs. Grieving over infertility and longing for that genetic link is normal.

When righteous Hannah experienced infertility, she wept bitterly, felt "greatly distressed," described herself as oppressed, and wouldn't eat. Notice that God does not say to her, "You shouldn't feel that way."

If infertility were an event, couples could grieve the loss and move on, but infertility is a process. Thus, grief may drag on for years. Many have described it as a roller coaster of hope and despair.[11]

Loss by Abortion

Abortion is another major form of child loss today. Whether the abortion was therapeutic or elective, abortion still involves the loss of a child and needs to be grieved. In our society, women are not encouraged to grieve over an abortion; they're supposed to be pleased and relieved rather than sad. That's not realistic.

Vicky Thorn of *Project Rachel* reports that women generally have not been helped by others' easy dismissal of guilt. "When women are told, 'Don't worry about it. You did the best you could under the circumstances. Get on with your life,' it hasn't proven helpful for them. They inwardly feel the abortion was wrong, and they want and need someone to be honest with them and say, 'Yes, it is wrong to take a baby's life.' They can then accept that fact and get on with mourning."[12]

The grief response for women who have abortions is often different from that for other types of loss. Some feel relief and happiness that it's over. But many repress and deny their real feelings of loss and guilt for a prolonged period. These emotions may not surface for years. I have seen this occur time and again in the counseling office. It's not just women who experience this loss; men experience it as well.

If you have experienced abortion or know someone who has, reach out and take the steps necessary for you or the other person to discover forgiveness and recovery through the grief process.

Loss by Adoption

Losing a child to adoption is one of the most significant losses birth parents will ever have to face.

When parents give up their baby to adoption, some were pressured to do so, while others felt it was the best step they could take for their child. For many birth parents, this is an ambiguous loss. Their child is alive but not present with them.

Today, open adoption is often presented to birth parents as a way to lessen the grief of losing a child to adoption. Ongoing contact with the child and the adoptive family is often portrayed in ideal terms. However, being able to see your child and even eventually develop a relationship with him or her does not change the fact that you are no longer the child's parent. In fact, the loss of being mom or dad is often painfully obvious with each visit, from the infant who will stop crying only when the adoptive mother picks him up, to the toddler who has become "Daddy's" little girl.

The grief the birth parent feels for her or his child includes not only missing the times of being the child's mother (or father), but also mourning the milestone times he or she will not experience with the child as a parent.

Some birth parents console themselves with the idea that the loss in an open adoption is really quite small. After all, they will be able to maintain contact and eventually have a relationship with their child. Some even go so far as to think about the adoption in only positive terms, denying there has been any loss at all.

Often, birth parents may deny the loss by directly avoiding it. They may fill their days with so much activity that they "don't have time" to grieve. They may also deliberately avoid places and people that remind them of their pregnancy, including the adoptive parents and their child. Occasionally, a birth parent may start abusing drugs or alcohol as a way of attempting to avoid the loss.

As the shock wears off, feelings of sorrow and depression will emerge. Feelings of loss and sadness will color the way a birth parent looks at the world. Everything seems to be a reminder of the child that is no longer hers.

It's again important to identify the specific losses and grieve each one. If you gave up your baby for adoption, you may be hoping that your child will choose to find you once he or she is an adult.

Some adoptive children do, and some don't. In various ways, you could be grieving this loss most of your life.

An important consideration is that birth fathers often grieve their loss differently than birth mothers. Unfortunately, most birth fathers are not involved in the decision-making process concerning their children. While the reasons for non-involvement vary, this often increases their feelings of helplessness and can result in further distancing themselves from the situation. Additionally, birth fathers often experience guilt for "not being able to provide" for their children.

The American Adoption Congress has a list of professionals who specialize in adoption.[13]

Stillbirth Loss

Stillbirth is a frequent form of loss—1 out of every 100 births—although the tendency is to believe it happens only to other families. When it occurs, it's more devastating than a miscarriage because the parents felt they had passed through the risky period and everything should have been all right. There has also been more time for bonding with the child. Everyone has been getting ready for the birth and the baby shower. Announcements have been purchased, prospective baby-sitters selected. But when the baby is born, there is no cry, no breath, no life. The parents are shocked into grief.

Once again, others will find it hard to help with the loss, because the baby didn't exist for them. The mother and father feel isolated, and when they're admonished to go on with life and plan for another child, they receive no encouragement to grieve. But they have a need and a right to grieve and to take whatever steps are necessary to do that.

I've talked with couples whose experience of stillbirth is all too common. Family members may strongly suggest that autopsies and funeral services be forgotten to make the loss easier for them. That approach actually makes it more difficult.

Parents question themselves and each other about what caused it. Carol Staudacher, in her book *Beyond Grief*, describes the ways that parents repeatedly analyze the pregnancy and birth:

Reviewing the Pregnancy

- What happened during my pregnancy that didn't happen to people with healthy babies? What did I do wrong?
- How many hours did I sleep each night? Did I sleep too much or too little? Should I have taken a nap in the afternoon?
- How many cigarettes did I have a day?
- How many cocktails did I have during my pregnancy?
- Did I run down the stairs or did I merely walk fast?
- Did I try to exercise too much? Didn't I get enough exercise?
- Should I have abstained from sexual intercourse?
- Did I think something that made the baby die?

Reviewing the Birth

- Did I select the wrong doctor?
- Did I go to the hospital too late in labor?
- Should I have refused an anesthetic?
- Should I not have attempted natural childbirth?
- Didn't I try hard enough?

The questions are varied and many, depending on your individual circumstances. As you continue to review the pregnancy and birth, you define the boundaries of what you perceive as having been your personal responsibility. You release some of the guilt and begin the long, slow process of fully acknowledging your loss. As long as guilt is the major issue, the baby cannot be relinquished. The baby is held onto with "If onlys." If only I hadn't run ... or stayed up the night before ... or eaten too much ... or cried too much ... or taken a diuretic ... and on and on.

Along with the guilt you inflict on yourself is the guilt you either assume or imagine coming from other people. For example, some husbands intentionally or inadvertently insinuate the child's life was in the wife's domain, thereby implying she should have prevented the death. Even the idle remarks of relatives or friends can reinforce existing guilt or produce new guilts. The father who says, "I told you to quit smoking!"; the sister who self-righteously proclaims, "My doctor told me not to drink at all during pregnancy, and I didn't"; the neighbor who asks, "Weren't you still working in your eighth month?" adds to your self-blame.[14]

Parents who suffer a stillbirth need to validate and confirm their child's existence by seeing, holding, touching, naming, praying over and burying their baby. When they don't, they are left with doubts that they actually had a child. One woman went to the market and weighed vegetables to find one the weight and height of her stillborn child that she had not been allowed to see or hold, which left her without the memory she needed.

Parents need to take steps to make the baby real to them. One such step is to review as a couple your thoughts and feelings about—and experiences with—the baby throughout the length of the pregnancy. It's also most helpful—whether the problem is an inability to conceive, a miscarriage or a stillbirth—to find a support group with others who have just gone through the same experience.[15]

Loss by Sudden Infant Death Syndrome

Newborn children die, and that's different from a stillbirth loss, because the parents have some time to know and bond with a living child. Their grief is similar to that of losing an older child. But some factors still hinder grief recovery. Others may downplay the child's death, and when a loss is discounted, grief work is hampered.

Why may others seem insensitive? Most people don't know anyone who has lost a newborn, so they don't know how to respond. They didn't know your baby and thus can't really join you emotionally in your grief. Even hospitals engage in "protective" behavior that hampers a mother's grief by moving her from the obstetric ward to another location so she will not be reminded of her experience.

Statements like these are never helpful: "You're fortunate you didn't have time to get really attached." "You can be glad you hadn't taken him home yet." They negate the fact of a parent's love and the bonding that already occurred. Sometimes before the mother had a chance to leave the hospital, friends and relatives go into her home and remove all indications that she would have had a baby there. The desire to shield her from the pain won't help her grieve.

One of the most stressful types of newborn death is sudden infant death syndrome (SIDS). It's the sudden and unexpected death of what appeared to be a healthy infant. The death remains unexplained, even after a thorough postmortem exam. This is a real medical dilemma. It's the largest cause of death among infants between the ages of two weeks and one year, with the greatest number of deaths occurring between two and four months.[16]

This problem is at least as old as Old Testament times and seems to have occurred as frequently in the eighteenth and nineteenth centuries as it does now. Is it possible to predict? No. Could it have been prevented by a physician? No. It's not caused by suffocation, neglect, aspiration or regurgitation, pneumonia, heart attack or changing modes of infant care. It isn't hereditary or contagious. It does appear to be more common, however, among the lower socioeconomic classes.

Many theories exist about the cause, but there are no answers.[17] Because SIDS strikes with the suddenness of an earthquake, without warning, these deaths devastate the remaining family members, generating an abundance of guilt and anger.

There's an overwhelming sense of shock and disbelief when a healthy infant is found dead. Then comes an unrestrained welling up of "No!" that cannot be shouted loud enough. This death seems impossible, for the last few hours before the baby was put to bed were normal. The baby didn't cry or otherwise indicate a problem; the baby went to bed so many times before and always woke up later. But this time was different.

The result is self-imposed guilt, blame and hate. "What did I do or not do that caused this? Where did I go wrong?" If the baby died in the care of someone else, such as a baby-sitter or relative, that person may have to face accusations about doing or failing to do something significant.

Because of the nature of SIDS, police, medical examiners or hospital personnel may investigate the death. Sometimes the parents, in the midst of their grief and guilt, have to deal with accusations from those investigators. And even when the official interrogation is concluded, parents continue to grill themselves, looking for a cause and a reason. As one parents said:

> You rehearse everything you did prior to the baby's death. You consider the clothing of the baby, the way the crib was prepared, the temperature of the room, what the baby ate or didn't eat. Was there a sigh, a cough, a cry, an irritability or dullness that escaped your notice? You may recall a gesture or a sound that, upon reflection, you decide was a signal of your baby's distress when, in fact, it is only a product of your desperate imagination.[18]

Parents who lose a child to SIDS are extremely vulnerable emotionally. There is no letup, and they usually have to explain the death of their baby over and over. "What did the baby die of? Weren't you home? How often did you check her? Did the baby choke? Smother?" All the repetitive questions increase guilt and anxiety. Delores Kuenning identifies yet another problem:

> Friends and family are often afraid to talk to parents—because they don't know what to say; they don't say anything. This adds to the SIDS parents' isolation.
> One mother said, "You feel so isolated within yourself. When people withdraw from you because of their own discomfort, in a way, it's almost like an accusation that you were at fault. You feel you must have done something wrong, or this wouldn't be happening to you. On the other hand, you almost feel like they don't want to be around you because they feel it might be catching. I know people don't know what to say. I would rather they'd come and be with me or ask permission, 'Would you like someone to be with you?' rather than feel, 'Well, I don't know what to say so I think I'll stay away.'"
> Another added, "Friends who have well babies often don't know what to do about visiting. Sometimes it is just too painful for the parents to see another baby right at that moment. Some SIDS parents find this painful for as long

as a year. I suggest the friend call and simply ask how the parents feel about seeing other babies."

The first mother *wanted* to see other children. "I wanted to see there were children out there who were living and laughing and okay. I needed to see and feel and hope that I could again have that someday. It is always better to ask how the parents feel than to assume they do or do not want to see other babies."[19]

When sudden death occurs, a parent may deny the baby died. A mother continues doing what she did before—functioning as the baby's parent. She may continue to clean and arrange the nursery, prepare formula or fix the baby's clothes. It's a denial to protect against the crushing ache of the loss. When the shock subsides, withdrawal is common from outsiders and even the family. Dreams may contain the theme of searching for, caring for and playing with the baby.

What is it like to experience this type of loss, whether it's miscarriage, stillbirth, SIDS, infertility or, in some cases, abortion? You may experience emotional numbing, rage, fearfulness, shame and even a continuing sense that you are pregnant.

These are all normal responses. Most of the crazy feelings of grief will be your companions.

> The degree of trauma following pregnancy loss or abortion varies considerably from case to case, but clearly the loss of a long-wished for and/or last-chance pregnancy generally involves a great deal more trauma than other pregnancy losses. Difficulty concentrating, thinking clearly, reading, sleeping, relaxing or eating for a period of time immediately following the crisis is neither abnormal or uncommon.[20]

In the early days and months, emotional numbing can be an anesthesia that protects you from the overwhelming loss.

If rage comes to the forefront of your emotions, there are a number people at whom you may direct it: your spouse, your doctor, nurses, hospital personnel, friends, family or your own body.

You may experience fearfulness, hopelessness and a feeling of vulnerability when you lose something so precious. The more irreplaceable the loss, the more you hurt.

When there is any kind of a reproductive loss, there could be feelings of remorse or shame or even a sense of being punished. Even self-condemnation may be a way to explain this loss. The feeling of shame can be especially present in an abortion and can stunt the healthy grief process.

As strange as it seems, a woman who has experienced this loss may "feel pregnant" for the duration of the pregnancy or forget she is no longer pregnant. There may be frequent dreams about the experience.

In any loss, you have to recognize and accept both the fact and the feelings. You'll live in the valley of loss for a portion of your life. Don't fight it. You can't. Face it and take charge of it. It's a step in recovery.

English academic C. S. Lewis, author of *Mere Christianity*, didn't marry until later in life. After just four years of marriage, his wife, Joy, died of cancer. In his book *A Grief Observed*, he wrote:

> I once read the sentence, "I lay awake all night with a toothache, thinking about the toothache and about lying awake." That's true to life. Part of every misery is, so to speak, the misery's shadow or reflection: the fact that you don't merely suffer but have to keep on thinking about the fact that you suffer. I not only live each endless day in grief, but live each day thinking about living each day in grief.[21]

Is Recovery Possible?

It's true that the awareness of how much you hurt can cause even greater hurt; but the realization that the hurt is not permanent can lessen it. It won't last forever, but it will come in waves, and you will feel a wave come crashing in unexpectedly from time to time. It's just like ocean waves hitting the shore. Afterward, there's a time of calm.

God does not allow us to experience more than we can handle, even if we feel otherwise. That is His promise to us (see 1 Cor. 10:13).

There are several steps you can take in the grieving process of this loss to walk toward recovery.

The Role of Memory

Working through the grief involves a number of steps. Remembrance is important and healthier than denial.

It means remembering all the details of the loss. It also includes remembering any dreams you had about this lost child, what your family would have been like with the addition of this child, as well as what kind of parent you would have been to the child. This kind of identification is necessary in order to say goodbye in a healthy manner.

The Role of Others' Support

If you've lost a child, keep in mind that the more you allow others to support and care for you, the sooner you'll recover. Christians don't detour around grief. They do have greater resources available to handle it, however. Let others help you, pray for you and love you. Tell your story as often as you need to. Listen to these comments from a survivor of a neonatal death, who is also a support-group facilitator:

> Every time you talk about it, every time you go through your story and talk about some part of the grief process, as painful as it might be at the moment, it becomes easier. Some people need to continue to talk about it a few times. Some people need to continue to talk about it over and over again. I felt the need for a long time to tell the sorry. At least a year.[22]

The Role of Ritual in "Letting Go"

One of the challenges at this time is to somehow make your loss more real and tangible. It helps the grieving process to be able to see what is lost; but in the case of many of these losses, it isn't possible. For many, rituals have been helpful, such as a funeral or memorial service, especially when it is held on significant dates. You can also express your hopes and dreams for your lost baby by writing a letter to the child expressing your dreams as well as naming your child. Reading your letter aloud at one of your ceremonies can be healing.

Some parents make a memorial or offering of some kind in honor of their child. This could be a plant or tree or a gift somewhere in honor of your child.

Letting go is part of the process of moving on in your grief. This could be you and others writing goodbye letters, attaching them to balloons and releasing them, putting notes in a river, burning medical records related to the loss, and so on.

I've mentioned this before throughout the book, but facing and expressing your feelings is a must. Yes, they are painful, but necessary, and they require expression.

You will also benefit from having a place where you can speak openly about your loss and be heard and accepted without others trying to fix you.[23]

Recovery will not mean a once-and-for-all conclusion to your grief, especially with any loss regarding a child. It's a twofold process: (1) regaining your ability to function as you once did, and (2) resolving and integrating your loss into your life.

Redefining Recovery

In a sense, you will never recover completely, because you'll never be exactly the way you were before the loss. Your loss changes you. As someone once asked in a counseling session, "If I can't be the way I was before, and I never recover completely, what is all this about recovery? I'm confused. What does it mean? How can you recover, but not fully?"

Recovery means you get your capabilities and attributes back so that you can use them. It means that you reach a point where you're no longer fighting your loss, but accepting it. Acceptance doesn't mean you would have chosen it or even that you like it, but you've learned to live with it as a part of your life. Recovery doesn't mean you don't mourn occasionally and watch out for holidays and special dates. It means you learn to go on with your life.

I still have a scar from an incision made during an operation when I was a child. It reminds me that I had that experience. Recovery is like a scar from an operation, but it's in such a sensitive place that on occasion you feel the ache again. You can't predict when it will happen. In writing this chapter and the preceding one, the ache returned for me several times.

Recovery means reinvesting in life. A newfound source of joy is possible. But you could very well feel uncomfortable with whatever is new. You may think that experiencing the joys of life again is somehow wrong. Besides, if you begin to hope or trust again, you could experience another loss.

I've talked to some people who never want another child or who distance themselves from their remaining children to protect themselves. But there still is life, and in the midst of sorrow there can be joy.

The Lord is the source of our joy. The psalmist stated that He "clothes us with joy." God extends to each of us the invitation to reinvest in life.[24]

> I will exalt you, O LORD, for you lifted me out of the depths and did not let my enemies gloat over me. O LORD my God, I called to you for help and you healed me. O LORD, you brought me up from the grave; you spared me from going down into the pit. Sing to the LORD, you saints of his; praise his holy name. For his anger lasts only a moment, but his favor lasts a lifetime; weeping may remain for a night, but rejoicing comes in the morning. When I felt secure, I said, "I will never be shaken." O LORD, when you favored me you made my mountain stand firm; but when you hid your face, I was dismayed. To you, O LORD, I called; to the Lord I cried for mercy: "What gain is there in my destruction, in my going down into the pit? Will the dust praise you? Will it proclaim your faithfulness? Hear, O LORD, and be merciful to me; O LORD, be my help." You turned my wailing into dancing; you removed my sackcloth and clothed me with joy, that my heart may sing to you and not be silent. O LORD my God, I will give you thanks forever (Ps. 30).

Did you notice what the psalm said about grief and recovery?
In grief, we sometimes feel like we're going to die.
In grief, we sometimes feel like God has hidden His face.

In grief, we also have times when we feel God has favored us. In recovery, we discover that weeping will not last forever!

What about you? Are there clothes of mourning that you would like to exchange for clothes of joy?

You don't usually have a choice in your loss, but you do have a choice in your recovery. The changes in your identity, relationships, new roles and even abilities can be either positive or negative.

I have seen people who choose to live in denial and move ahead as though nothing has really happened. I have seen people stuck in the early stages of their grief who choose to lead lives of bitterness and blame. Some become so hardened and angry that it's difficult to be around them. They've made a choice. Life is full of losses, but you have the choice of doing something constructive or destructive with your loss. It's not the fault of other people or God.

Are there any criteria you can use in the grieving process to evaluate whether recovery is occurring for you? Yes, there are. It often helps, however, to go through such an evaluation with a person who can give you an objective viewpoint.

Dr. Therese Rando has made an outstanding contribution to the study of grief and recovery.[25] She suggests that recovery should be seen by observing changes in yourself, in your relationship with what you lost, and in your relationship with the world and other people. As you read and answer the following evaluation based on Dr. Rando's work, the conclusions you reach may help you decide where you are in your recovery.[26]

On a scale of 0 to 10 (0 meaning "not at all" and 10 meaning "total recovery in that area"), rate yourself in response to each question. This evaluation is geared toward the loss of a person, but it can be adapted to other losses as well.

I have returned to normal levels of functioning in most areas of my life.

0————————————5————————————10

My overall symptoms of grief have declined.

0————————————5————————————10

My feelings do not overwhelm me when I think about my loss or someone mentions it.

0————————————————5————————————————10

Most of the time, I feel all right about myself.

0————————————————5————————————————10

I enjoy myself and what I experience without feeling guilty.

0————————————————5————————————————10

My anger has diminished, and when it occurs, it is handled appropriately.

0————————————————5————————————————10

I don't avoid thinking about things that could be or are painful.

0————————————————5————————————————10

My hurt has diminished, and I understand it.

0————————————————5————————————————10

I can think of positive things.

0————————————————5————————————————10

I have completed what I need to do about my loss.

0————————————————5————————————————10

My pain does not dominate my thoughts or my life.

0————————————————5————————————————10

I can handle special days or dates without being totally overwhelmed by memories.

0————————————————5————————————————10

I can remember the loss on occasion without pain and crying.

0————————————————5————————————————10

There is meaning and significance to my life.

0————————————5————————————————10

I am able to ask *how* rather than *why* at this time.

0————————————5————————————————10

I see hope and purpose in life in spite of my loss.

0————————————5————————————————10

I have energy and can feel relaxed during the day.

0————————————5————————————————10

I no longer fight the fact that the loss has occurred. I have accepted it.

0————————————5————————————————10

I am learning to be comfortable with my new identify and in being without what I lost.

0————————————5————————————————10

I understand that my feelings over the loss will return periodically and I can accept that.

0————————————5————————————————10

I understand what grief means and have a greater appreciation for it.

0————————————5————————————————10

Changes in My Relationship with the Person I Lost

I remember our relationship realistically, with positive and negative memories.

0————————————5————————————————10

My relationship with the person I lost is healthy and appropriate.

0————————————5————————————————10

I feel all right about not thinking about the loss for a time. I am not betraying the one I lost.

0————————————5————————————10

I have a new relationship with the child I have lost. I know appropriate ways of keeping my child alive in my memories.

0————————————5————————————10

I no longer go on a search for my loved one.

0————————————5————————————10

I don't feel compelled to hang on to the pain.

0————————————5————————————10

The ways I keep my loved one alive are healthy and acceptable.

0————————————5————————————10

I can think about things in life other than what I lost.

0————————————5————————————10

My life has meaning even though this person is gone.

0————————————5————————————10

Changes I Have Made in Adjusting to My New World

I have integrated my loss into my world, and I can relate to others in a healthy way.

0————————————5————————————10

I can accept the help and support of other people.

0————————————5————————————10

I am open about my feelings in other relationships.

0————————————5————————————10

I feel it is all right for life to go on even though my loved one is gone.

0————————————————5————————————————10

I have developed an interest in people and things outside myself that have no relationship to the person I lost.

0————————————————5————————————————10

I have put the loss in perspective.

0————————————————5————————————————10

Isaiah said that God "shall be the stability of your times" (Isa. 33:6, *NASB*). His presence in our lives will enable us to recover.

RECOMMENDED READING

- Debra Bridwell, *The Ache for a Child*
- Donna Gibbs, Becky Garrett and Phyllis Rabon, *Water from the Rock: Finding God's Comfort in the Midst of Infertility*
- Sandra L. Glahn and William R. Cutrer, *When Empty Arms Become a Heavy Burden: Encouragement for Couples Facing Infertility*
- John MacArthur, *Safe in the Arms of God: Truth from Heaven about the Death of a Child*
- Jennifer Saake, *Hannah's Hope: Seeking God's Heart in the Midst of Infertility*
- John and Sylvia Van Regenmorter, *When the Cradle Is Empty: Coping with Infertility*
- Kathe Wunnenberg, *Grieving the Child I Never Knew*

7

The Disabled Child

When we think of losing a child, we usually think of death first; but there are many other ways to experience the loss of a child even when he or she continues to live.

A child who is disabled—whether the affliction results from an accident, disease, deformity, mental illness or any other cause—is prevented from being all that he or she could be. There are times when the disability isn't visible or apparent, but it is there all the same. And no matter what type of disability exists, a disabled child is a lifetime of loss.

When you know at your child's birth that something is wrong, in order to survive this disruption of life, you have to grieve the loss of normalcy, the life you knew and the life you dreamed for your child and you. Do you remember your first response at the news? The discovery of a disability can be as traumatic as death. I've been there in the doctor's office to hear the diagnosis when our family's life was shattered.

Our son, Matthew, was disabled and died at the age of 22. At that time, he was only 18 months old mentally. This is how my wife described our life:

Matthew was nine months old when I saw his first grand mal seizure. His entire body stiffened, his arms and legs jerked uncontrollably, and his eyes rolled back in his head. Seeing a convulsion in your child for the first time is terrifying! We were outside with a neighbor, and I had no clue what to do. The only thing I could think to do was to pray with my eyes open, in Jesus' name, while cradling Matthew in my arms. I felt *utterly helpless*. I will never forget that day, though I've often wished I could. Finally, the seizures stopped, and I thanked God it was over.

Norm was away at Green Oaks Boys Camp training counselors. When he rushed home in response to my emergency call, I blurted out, "Why weren't you with me? Why weren't you here when we needed you?" He looked so puzzled and vulnerable. I could see my question was unreasonable, because the seizure lasted only a few minutes. From then on, I realized that when a seizure did come, I was not alone. It was the Lord, Matthew and me.

Gradually, my confidence and faith were built up as we three weathered each episode. In the past, I had been a very dependent wife, so I needed to learn to be more independent when Norm was busy or away in his ministry. The Lord was obviously refining me to be the wife and mother He wanted me to be.

Matthew had more seizures, so we placed him under the care of neurologists at UCLA Medical Center. After extensive testing, the doctor told us, "For some reason, something happened with the development of Matthew's brain, and that accounts for the severity of the retardation. And then at birth, further brain damage occurred somehow, which accounts for the seizure condition. Matthew may develop into a two-year-old mentally someday, and then again, he may not."

What is your experience? Perhaps you've had a child with disabilities for years, or maybe it's a recent diagnosis. Where are you in your grief? There are different phases, or states, that most people in grief experience.

Phases of Grieving for a Disabled Child

Your expectations are disrupted if not crushed. It's a different type of grief. As a parent you are numb, shocked, angered; you struggle with grief because your child is not dead, but alive. This loss is different

from the loss of death. There are no rituals for the grieving process,
nor a ceremonial period of mourning to end the grieving process,
for there is no ending. Some of your losses are perceived, intangible
and threatened, yet they are still losses all the same. And the losses
begin to dominate and control your life and how you live.

It is normal for an abundance of feelings to rage out of control. Some describe it as the "collapsing effect." This includes an
abundance of fatigue and then depression, anxiety and the sense of
being overwhelmed. Within this is a buildup of sadness and disappointment, creating a mood that is difficult to change. One mother
said, "I can tell you why I feel overwhelmed. It's when I have tried
everything and every solution has been tried and exhausted—where
do I go from there? My life seems to shrink each day."

I saw this in my wife, Joyce, as our mentally disabled son,
Matthew, grew older. The week following his placement, at age 11,
others commented, "It's as though a 100-pound weight was lifted
from Joyce."

Some people are able to keep their child with them their entire
life. Others are led to place their child in a facility, which can provide
better care than they could receive at home. That is what we did.

After Matthew's placement at Salem Christian Home. I experienced an incredible lifting of my spirit, because I was
released from the physical demands of the care. I slept like
never before, felt well and looked around at my world with
wonder and awe. I now had the opportunity for my personality to develop and blossom. For 11 years, it was as if I had
taken a detour from life to carry a heavy but very special
responsibility, and I needed to reorient myself to life.

Before long, we could see that Matthew was well, gain-
ing weight, and in school more consistently. When he visited us at home, he seemed brighter and more alert. Life was
obviously more meaningful for him.

He learned so much at Salem! He learned to walk up
stairs, turn on a faucet, dog paddle in a pool and feed himself. (Three bites out of five hitting the mouth aren't bad!)
He didn't forget us, and he maintained his good-natured
disposition. He seemed to enjoy music, and now and then

he would sit at the piano and bang on the keys. Occasionally, he would throw his head back and clap his hands.

One of our more precious gifts from Matthew was his learning to hug. For 15 years, we never received any response when we held him. We realized he was limited because his mental development never seemed to progress beyond an 18-month-old level. But something happened, and occasionally when we hugged him—perhaps two or three times a year—we would feel his arms around us in return. And sometimes when we would look at him, open our arms, and say, "Matthew, hug," he would come to us with arms open in response. You can't imagine how we valued those responses.

Feelings of Denial

If you went through denial or you're still there, you're normal. You think, *This isn't (can't be, must not be) happening to me and my child.* There is a resounding no to what has disturbed and disrupted your life.

Of course you experience denial. We all do. There are some positives to this response. It can buy you some time to discover some inner strength. It can help you from falling apart until you find the resources you need to cope. Your denial is like Novocain and helps you make the amount of pain bearable.

Feelings of Anger and Fear

And then the anger arrives, looking for its target upon which to land. That anger is grief talking, and it's a sign of frustration in searching for a reason for the disability as well as an elusive solution.

As if this is not enough, a new intruder enters your life—fear—fear of the unknown, the future, distress or disorder. What were your fearful questions? Most parents at first hope for the best, but in their heart and mind they fear the worst. We tend to expect the worst. The "what ifs" come into play about the child, his future, your future, and they never seem to end.

Other fears include society's rejection, fears about how brothers and sisters will be affected, questions as to whether there will be any more brothers or sisters in this family, and concerns about whether the husband or wife will love this child. These fears can almost immobilize some parents.

You may worry about not giving meds on time or missing appointments, or your child's future or how others will respond to him, and finances or what will happen to your child if you're not around. One mother said, "My greatest ongoing fear for me and my child is the fear of emotional pain."

Feelings of Confusion

With any loss there is confusion. With the diagnosis comes new information and medical terminology that may be difficult to understand. It's difficult to make sense of what is said and sometimes the medical staff isn't quite sure. You're facing mental overload; and at a time when you're thinking ability has been compromised, you need to learn about something new and devastating and make wise decisions, which is asking a lot. Some parents retreat and isolate themselves, as well as their child.

Feelings of Powerlessness

If you're like me, you prefer to be in control and capable, and when you're not, you struggle. This, too, is another loss. With a disabled child you often feel powerless. Now you have to rely upon those who know more and have opinions and recommendations for your child. You're the parent and the one who is supposed to decide what's best for your child, but now that's being done by strangers.

Feelings of Guilt

Guilt and blame seep in. There's self-blame, which generates guilt; but there's another way you might try to deal with this—you might blame your spouse's family heritage. There's a genetic defect on his or her side. "My spouse is responsible for this. It's not my side of the family."

Stages of Adjustment

As with any loss, we work toward a level of acceptance. This doesn't mean liking it, but realizing this is what we have, and we will grow through the experiences. Acceptance will have its own set of complications.

Since the child continues to live and to require the parents to constantly adapt to meet his extraordinary needs, grief is ongoing and parental wounds are often unable to heal. The loss is a living loss, a loss without a foreseeable end.

Even after you've found acceptable ways to cope with your child and his or her life by accepting the disability, other complications can cause setbacks in adjustment.

Dealing with Others' Negativity

What about the unanticipated experiences of being socially rebuffed by friends and strangers, or being treated inappropriately by poorly informed educators or therapists? Such repeated negative experiences only aggravate the difficult process of remaining in the highest stage of adjustment.

We, like professionals, readily perceive the inhumanity of persons who show little or no understanding or caring toward children with disabilities or their caretakers. Peoples' actions, more frequently than events, cause parents and their child to regress to earlier stages of feelings and behaviors. Most of us need assistance to progress positively and without being sidetracked through the stages of adjustment. Progress toward a level of reasonable acceptance, closure and reconstruction includes an accurate understanding of reality, at least as we reach the usual and customary benchmarks in our child's development.

While most of us want and have a need for professionals to be truthful as a prerequisite to being recognized as trustworthy persons with credibility, we do not need information that is bleak and replete with dismal prognosis; and not every parent may experience these stages of grief, suffering and acceptance.[1]

Experiencing Traumatic Life Changes

When you discover that your child is disabled, your mind may not grasp what this means or what the future holds. You won't be able to equip your child for a normal life; and the control you want, to handle the overwhelming loss, is nonexistent. All losses impact us, but this is beyond comprehension. The world as you know it and expected it to be is gone—vanished, destroyed. For many, this isn't just a loss. Their values have been shattered; but their inability to handle it is not their fault.

It's a non-recognized traumatic event that changes your entire life and, at first, not for the better. Your life with others has shrunk as your child's needs consume you. Many parents I have worked with reflect three words, to one degree or another: *disillusionment, discouragement* and *despair*. All of these are beyond the normal range of intensity. The chronic sorrow you experience leaves you with the feeling of being alone, since few others understand what you and your child are experiencing. One mother said, "I walk into a room of parents that I know, and I feel alone. I can't connect. And neither can they."

Bargaining for a Cure

There is a long-running television show titled *Let's Make a Deal*. You probably saw it at one time or another. The search and wish for a solution or healing drives us. Did you look for a miracle cure? Many do. Or if you work harder with your child, your child could improve. You look for new deals. Some "shop" for a new diagnosis and prognosis. The right professional, the right school or procedure or program will solve the problem. Bargaining with God can fall into this stage.

Living with Chronic Sorrow

When reality can no longer be denied, when angry energy does not change the child's condition, and when there are no more deals to be made, a sense of depression sets in. Sadness grips the heart as a reality that must be dealt with. The truth is extremely painful and often overwhelming. During this period, parents may question the meaning of life and their value as human beings. Because of the intense grief and shame, they may avoid others with typical children.

Sorrow is the natural response that has been waiting in the wings while we go through the other stages.[2]

One of your tasks at this time is letting go of your dream for a "normal" child. You'll accomplish this when you come to an understanding of the uniqueness of this child, just like you learn to understand and accept the uniqueness of every other child. Do you view your child as a child, or as a disability? Your child is first of all still a child. Yes, you will probably always have to live in uncertainty about the present and future. And the losses will always be with you.

And so is something else: an intense sorrow that has its own special name.

Chronic sorrow, a normal grief response, is not the same as grief at the finality of death, where the person who is loved will be forever absent. Chronic sorrow is not about endings; it is about living with unresolvable loss and wounds that do not entirely heal. It is about losses requiring—and demanding—energy and persistent courage to cope with crises, and making the adaptations necessary in order to live a life of one's own. It is about year upon year of dealing with the inevitability of a loss that continues, and of finding a way to achieve some balance between reality and losing one's grip entirely.[3]

Loss becomes your constant and unwelcome companion.

Dr. Robert Naseef, a parent of a disabled child, describes a common experience: "For all parents, a child's birth is a time of great joy and optimism. 'Your child has a disability' is one of the most crushing statements that one can ever hear. Your child can be the source of great joy or devastating sorrow. No matter whether the disability is mild or severe it crushes you for a while and you probably tend to hope for the best, but imagine the worst."[4]

Dr. Naseef goes on to say:

> There are different incidences or odds for each disability, but when it happens to you, it's always 100%. You are totally surrounded by your fate, as the father played by Nick Nolte in the movie *Lorenzo's Oil* highlighted when he said that he felt like "a loser in the genetic lottery."[5]

When people decide to have children, there is typically great joy at the impending life they are bringing into the world. But that elation and hope for the future can come to a crashing halt when a baby is born with a disability. For many, this is too much to bear, and sorrow and grief begin as the realization of lost hopes and dreams set in. Often parents of newborns with severe disabilities are advised to institutionalize their baby or risk destroying their marriage.[6] How do you handle this?

Being the parent of a disabled child is a lifetime of stress. If you're a parent of a disabled child, you probably understand the feeling of being depleted. As you give and give, there comes a time where you're running on empty, especially if this has gone on for years. And as you move into your senior years with less energy and income, your struggle increases.

One major stressor is the lack of time and space in which to sort through all the feelings as well as grieve. There is the loss of the dream you had for this child, but how do you grieve when the child still exists and demands more care than the other children? Not only that, the sacrificial care you give is often unrecognized, unappreciated and never seems to be enough. You don't receive back the love and warmth from this child as you do from others. With many disabled children, they change. Their condition may improve or they may deteriorate.

Or what if your child was healthy at first, and then the disease or disorder or accident occurred? You are plunged into deep loss but there is little understanding. Making decisions is difficult and often induces guilt. Sometimes the guilt is caused by anger directed toward the child who changed and changed your life. It's not his or her fault for changing, but you wish your child was back the way he or she used to be. The roller-coaster ride some parents are on is because their child is on one with the disability. For example, a child with autism may move forward one week, making healthy contact with eyes, but that disappears the next day. One day your child speaks with clarity and the next day cannot be understood. You're plunged from the mountaintop to the desert valley.[7]

Fantasies and dreams can be fulfilled. They can also be ruined. Your child may be a repository for your hopes and dreams and continuation of your family line and future. My family line stopped with my son. For many, becoming a parent is part of who they are, their personal identity. Men, and women especially, have spent years dreaming about their child and the joys of parenting. Many have stated that their imagined child was a part of their life, and perhaps the dreams were somewhat unrealistic. When you discover either immediately or in time that your child is disabled, your loss is not so much about the child you have, but it's about the child you dreamed of having. The impairment has changed not just your child but your hopes and future and dreams.

Because of their dreams, which have crumbled, there is a sense in many parents of not accepting the disability, whatever it may be, and the situation. It's not bad not to accept, for this can be a source of energy to help fight the situation and deal with future challenges. This is better than hopelessness, passive acceptance or a sense of total defeat.[8]

One struggle that most parents deal with is obtaining the care and help they believe their child needs. You have to be a persistent advocate for your child. I remember when I was nine and had some difficulties with a leg and my lower back, and I remained out of school for a semester. My mother took me to doctor after doctor until the tenth doctor was able to determine that I had a slight case of polio, which still existed back then. Fortunately, there were no lasting effects, but my mother's persistence was a must.

One father whose son needed residential care described what it's like to have to prove that your child has such a need and is eligible and has a right for the funding:

> I was to discover firsthand after reaching this painful conclusion, most people have to fight a legal battle to get this care for their child and a reasonable life for the rest of their family.
>
> Every tear drained out of my heart for months. Having to prove that my infant was damaged enough to deserve this care seemed like torture. Likewise, the average parent of a child with special needs must often struggle long and hard to get the best possible services for his or her child.[9]

Life in a Family with a Disabled Child

What is it like for a family adjusting to a child's disability?

The truth is, when a child with a disability becomes part of a family, the tensions begin to mount, and it is too easy for couples to find fault with each other and dump guilt on each other. The anxieties often begin to grow from the moment parents get the news.

Many losses are hard to deal with, but the loss of your child in this way causes mental torment. There is no one right way to grieve. It doesn't make sense despite explanations. Your dream is gone and your grief is "disenfranchised" because it's hard to openly acknowledge and publicly mourn this type of loss. Few people acknowledge it.

Living with a child who has special needs can be like living inside a pressure cooker. The less the child is able to function, the greater stress on every other family member. The expenditure of both physical and psychic energy is so great that everyone tends to be on a short fuse.

On the other hand, some couples speak of their experience in coping with a child with a disability as bonding them closer together, making their marriage stronger and firmer, building on the commitment to each other that was there in the first place.[10]

Not only has there been the loss of the "normal" child, but there are unknown aspects of this loss that impact the grief of the family members.

Disability is never as clear-cut as death. Grief usually mingles with confusion and uncertainty. Parents of a Down syndrome child may be told little beyond the label and have no idea what degree of retardation to expect. As they learn more, either through their own research or through professional consultation, the picture changes. As the child grows, he or she changes, too, often invalidating earlier predictions. Not knowing what fate to mourn, the parent faces a thousand alternative scenarios.[11]

Other Children in the Family

Siblings are impacted in many ways. Sorrow and anger are common emotions, and with good reasons, but often these feelings lead to guilt.

Siblings experience the profound unfairness that is part of their daily life. Their families must live with blindness, autism, retardation, schizophrenia, debilitating disease or cerebral palsy while other families are unscathed. They must take care of themselves as best they can and also take care of their sibling when they are very young, even before they start to school, while they see their peers avoiding most responsibilities throughout childhood. They notice that most of the family's available money and time are going to treatment, care and services for their disabled sibling.[12]

Sometimes they find their own possessions taken or destroyed by a disabled sibling who is out of control. Some learn not to become too attached to possessions, for who knows when they could be gone for one reason or another. Many learn that their needs will probably come last, and sometimes not at all. As one sibling described his life, "I've learned not to expect too much since my brother's needs have to come first. It's not his fault, but I feel let down so much. We plan a vacation and now I expect it to be cancelled or postponed. It's the way it is. Life is not fair."[13]

Too often when there is a disabled child, no one thinks about talking to the other children about what's going on and why. Consequently, they continue to struggle with their feelings, questions and pain. They may feel alone and even quite angry. They may respond in many ways, especially if they feel neglected.

You may not see much of a noticeable change in your other children. Or you may see a very positive change as a child decides to be overly good as her means of survival. She makes few demands on her exhausted and stressed parents, and she tries to be helpful. But she, too, has needs her parents have to meet, and she also requires an opportunity to grieve.

Many children hide their distress and have to deal with it years later, in adulthood. But another common reaction is to employ attention-getting mechanisms, such as rebelling, and especially if the child is disabled. It's the only way they know to recapture their parents' attention. If their attempts are ignored or discounted, they could intensify their efforts in this direction by using drugs, running away, setting fires, destroying property, and so on. Expressed anger is one way to gain attention.[14]

Children raised with a disabled sibling often feel a strong sense of responsibility, either self-imposed or placed there by the parents. Dr. Charlotte Thompson tells the story of a pediatrician who grew up with a disabled sibling. The family knew something was wrong with her brother, but the problem wasn't diagnosed until he was 15. He wasn't expected to do chores or have outside jobs like the other children. The parents had time and money for him, but very little for the others. They put up with temper tantrums and angry explosions from him, but they wouldn't tolerate any expression of anger from the others.

The disabled child knew he was favored and used it to his advantage. He ended up being viewed as the good child, and the others as the bad ones.

Eventually, the problem was diagnosed and a tumor was removed; but by now the family's finances were depleted. During that time, the other children never voiced their concern over the unfairness. When this pediatrician was in counseling for her marriage, here's what her therapist told her:

You've been carrying your brother on your back all of your life, which is probably one of the reasons you went into pediatrics. You have been trying to understand what happened with your brother and why you always felt him around your neck like a millstone. You have a highly over-developed sense of responsibility toward other children and have tried to mother the world. This has caused emotional problems, marital problems, and has left you feeling drained, angry and incomplete. Essentially you have had to be your own parent, and after your parents died, you felt a tremendous responsibility for your brother. By transferring his dependence from your parents to you, you created a very difficult problem for yourself. You may well know that people often grow to dislike, or even hate, close individuals on whom they feel dependent. This surely is your brother's case. First he hated your parents, now he hates you.[15]

That situation could have been avoided if the parents had communicated with the other children and had all worked together as a team. But who helps parents deal with their grief and gives them guidelines for responding to the other children? Usually no one does, which is why you need the assistance of other parents who have gone through the same struggles.

You may be aware that you're not doing what you want or need to with the other children. Your grief drains your energy and the emotional investment you want to make in them. Or you feel you're not being the parent you want to be, which adds to your frustration and sense of failure. But during the onset of the crisis with your child, it's unrealistic to think you can act the way you want with the other children. You just don't have enough to give.

You will also fluctuate in your feelings and responses to your children. You may feel resentment that your other children are healthy or still living, don't seem to be as concerned or grieve enough, or have adjusted too soon. Part of your response is your anger over the unfairness of what has happened. You may feel you can't invest what you want, or you've lost your ability to give. Or you may be afraid to invest because something bad could happen to these children. You could also overreact and over-protect. Being aware of these difficulties may help you to avoid them.[16]

Research has provided us with helpful information about what to expect and what might be avoided:

- Older siblings adjust better than younger children do to having a brother or sister with disabilities, with the exception of the eldest daughter, who doesn't adjust well.
- Eldest daughters are often given the task of caring for the child with special needs, much more often than are any other children in the family.
- Children are more affected by having a sibling with a disability if that sibling is of the same gender.
- If there are only two children in the family, and if the non-disabled sibling is a girl, she suffers more adverse effects.
- If there are only two children in the family, and one has a disability, the other is more pressured to fulfill the parents' hopes and dreams for success in their children. If the non-disabled child is a girl, she is also assigned more care-giving responsibilities.
- Siblings of children with disabilities tend to show positive qualities of being well adjusted, mature beyond their years, tolerant of differences in people, helpful toward people and aware of social needs.
- Siblings can be excellent teachers of their brother or sister with disabilities because they are in a different position in the family.
- Siblings may experience guilt as they surpass a disabled younger brother or sister in skills and abilities.
- The siblings may feel pressure to overachieve.
- Siblings may over-identify with a mildly disabled brother or sister, or may as they reach teen years not consider a severely disabled sibling a person.
- Siblings may feel that requests by parents for help with the brother or sister with a disability are an intrusion on their time or they may view it as a privilege to cooperate with the parents.[17]

It's interesting that choosing a helping profession as a vocation is common among the siblings of disabled people. Sometimes they carry guilt, feelings of responsibility or a sense of chronic sorrow or sadness into adulthood. Sometimes the acceptance of a disabled brother or sister gets harder as kids grow older. As a daughter of some friends put it, "I grow older and change. But my sister stays the same, and at times it seems as though she goes backward. She's an adult like I am, but I'm a real adult, and she's still in infancy. And she always will be. That's sad."

Siblings face numerous pressures we don't even think about. What does a child say to others when asked about a younger brother who just died?

What does a child say to others when asked about a sibling who doesn't look disabled in any way but is nonverbal?

Sometimes the *less severe* the impairment, the more difficult it is for the siblings, since they may feel embarrassed about their brother's or sister's behavior.

A family with a disabled child faces issues few others can even imagine, which calls for exceptional coping skills.

Perhaps this is your story. Families with disabilities often lose their privacy because they may deal with a number of professional helpers who come and go. Various private or state assistance agencies may get involved, and strangers come and go as well as know the intimate details of the family. Advice and treatment from so many different professionals may be contradictory. Family members may even get displaced from their rooms.

Life for everyone becomes abnormal, and there doesn't seem to be much of an escape since some disabilities will require permanent adjustment. But out of this, family members learn to adjust, grow, love and serve and become more than they ever could be without their disabled child. I know. My retarded son changed and enhanced my life because of who he was and by his presence.[18]

An individual is considered to have a disability if there is a physical or mental impairment that substantially limits one or more major life activities: seeing, hearing, speaking, walking, breathing, performing manual tasks, learning, caring for oneself, and working.

Many are surprised by how many children are disabled. About 3 percent of all children born in the United States have a birth defect.[19] One in 12 U.S. children are considered disabled either mentally or physically, and special education enrollment during the 1990s rose twice as fast as overall school enrollment.[20]

According to the March of Dimes, about 150,000 babies are born with birth defects each year in the United States. The American college of Obstetricians and Gynecologists (ACOG) says that 3 out of every 100 babies born in the United States have some kind of major birth defect.[21]

In addition to the stress of the disability itself, financial strain due to medical bills or quality care, lack of control over what life has dealt, egos, attitudes, isolation, anger, embarrassment, grief and protectiveness—all merge to bombard the family of a child with a disability. Without a safety net in the family, crises may loom.

These types of continuous challenges can be a reaction to the disability itself, the stress and strain the disability creates within the family unit, or a family member's reaction to the child with the disability. Regardless of the type of disability, parents must learn to cope with the fact that their child will never fulfill the life they had hoped and dreamed for them. The journey is long, and many families will not make it together.

Coping with Marital Strain

When a marriage relationship is unstable, the stress of dealing with a child's disability can cause the family system to collapse; on the other hand, in a relationship that is strong and relatively unstressed, a child's disability may develop increased closeness and strength in the parents' marriage. While there is a general impression that parents who have a child with a disability are more likely to split up than parents of "normal" children, there has been limited research in this area, and it is inconclusive.

Grandparents can have as hard a time accepting a disability as a parent. My mother did. Often you could see the pain in her eyes. Grandparents experience their own grief as well as grief for their own child, and often the grief of their disabled grandchild if the child is aware of his or her condition. Grandparents can struggle with guilt that they can't do enough to help. They may have passed on a defective gene and perhaps it appears again.

They also struggle with the loss of the dreams they had for the relationship with their grandchild.

There are a number of critical stress and intensified grief times when raising a disabled child. Some of these are connected to developmental steps or milestones, which are the ages at which you would expect your child to accomplish certain skills under normal circumstances. These milestones are walking, talking, going to school, the onset of puberty, and a child's twenty-first birthday. Each lack intensifies your grief. Not only are these missed milestones difficult, but also there are other factors that generate additional losses. Perhaps you have experienced these as well.

1. The initial diagnosis—I can still hear the words of the neurologist more than 40 years ago: "The best I can tell you is that Matthew's brain did not develop normally, which accounts for the severity of the mental retardation. At birth, for some reason, there was brain damage, which accounts for his grand mal seizures. The best I can tell you is that Matthew might become a two-year-old mentally. Then on the other hand, he might not." It's as though I was standing on the outside of myself, watching this interaction.
2. When younger siblings develop and pass their older sibling, his or her deficit stands out more.
3. Many families will face the possibility of placement. Some will consider it and decide not to for a number of reasons, while others will decide it is the wisest and best step to take.
4. The health problems that many disabled children have drain you of time, energy and finances. They may be occasional, but many experience them constantly. This can include being overly susceptible to any disease, as well as multiple seizures.
5. One major stressor most prefer to avoid is facing what might happen in the future when you as parents die. Guardianship and future care need to be faced, but like all of these issues, they can bring greater pain.[22]

Having a disabled child means that dreams are shattered, deferred or discarded. But some dreams are remade when expectations are given up, altered and reshaped. One father said, "We had to change our life, more than you'll ever know. We learned to love our children in the moment rather than in our dreams for them. And in loving them in the moment, the joy can come back into your life."

There is no question that the arrival of a child with a disabling condition can create great stresses in a family or intensify those stresses already present. And it can drive couples apart. But on the evidence of parents' experiences, this is not always the case:

- A family with a child who has a disability does not have to be a handicapped family.
- "It is not the child's disability that handicaps and disintegrates families; it is the way they react to it and to each other."[23]
- A family with a child who has special needs and requires special care does not have to disintegrate under stress.
- It is not the child's disability that handicaps and disintegrates families; it is the way they react to it—and to each other.
- Finding a way to deal with the added stresses, finding a way to minimize them and overcome them—by sharing them—can glue a marriage (and a family) together more firmly than ever.[24]

The Parents Who Are Survivors

No matter how seriously your child is disabled, you will make it if you learn to focus on what your child is able to do. A child will, in time, accomplish something he or she has never done before. It may be insignificant to others, but not to you.

Talk about what you are feeling. Reach out to people who are knowledgeable and supportive. You can join a support group, alleviating the isolation that so many experience as a result of having a child who is different from his or her peers.

Keep a journal of your thoughts. Although not everyone feels comfortable writing, it is a healthy way to express feelings of loss and grief and then read aloud what you've written.

Make time for yourself. Don't compromise your physical and emotional wellbeing. You may struggle with this, but it's necessary when you're a caregiver.

Seek help when needed. Help can come from family, friends, community organizations, respite care, health care professionals, the Internet or any other available and appropriate resource.

Learn how to redirect focus. Often you may feel as if you will never smile again; you will never again laugh or enjoy life. You can challenge this viewpoint with the question, "Of what value will that be to my child?"

We laughed a lot with Matthew. Here's how my wife described our life:

One of our funny episodes was quite frustrating at the time! Matthew and I were home sick from church on a Sunday, and Norm and Sheryl were still away. I did what I tended to do frequently and locked myself out of the house. (I have keys everywhere now.) Still in my robe, I was on my way to the garage with another load of diapers for the washer. I tried the door. It wouldn't open. I saw the dog; he was licking Matthew's face. And Matthew was serenely chewing on a bar of soap in his zip-up sleeper!

Another time, we had guests for dinner, and I had fixed a dessert with blueberries and cream on top of the glass dessert dish. Matthew ambled by Norm's uncle, and since no one was watching, he reached out and swept the top of that dessert off the dish and into his mouth. Many times, he outsmarted the dog and cat and ate their food as well!

On another occasion, the cat was asleep in the recliner. Matthew walked up and grabbed its tail with a viselike grip. The cat immediately came alive, leapt from the chair and ran full speed across the room. Matthew forgot to let go, and the cat literally dragged him across the room. His laughter rang through the house with his free ride.

Perhaps the following information gleaned from a seminar for parents and what they want and need from their spouse may connect with what you are experiencing:

What women need:

1. Women have it harder because they need more practical help in the everyday things. It's just too much to handle. A nanny would be ideal, but a teenager to help out for a few hours a day with child care or household chores would be great.
2. Women need more understanding and compassion from their husbands. We need to communicate more and listen to how they feel.
3. Women want to talk about other things, too, not just the child with the disability.
4. Women need more physical help when the man is home: they're worn out from the everyday grind.
5. Women want men to play with the child with special needs more and get to know more about him or her.
6. Women want men to take the children out and give the women some free time for herself.
7. Women want men to assume more responsibility around the house.
8. Women want men to pay more attention to how the woman is feeling and what she might need or want each day.

Women wanted the following:

1. The men to be involved in the child's education; they were tired of going to the meetings alone; they wanted the men to try, whenever possible, to take a few hours off from work to be with them at these times.
2. Some time alone to relax without the children.
3. To be able to talk about their feelings without the men getting defensive.
4. Time together as a couple.
5. Men to develop a better understanding of their child's special needs and not leave it all to the women.

What men wanted:

1. We want the women to understand that we are trying to help in the way we know how and that we're frustrated when we can't make things better.
2. We need more time as a couple again, to be together without the children.
3. We want women to be more rational and less emotional so that we can discuss problems and find solutions.
4. Let us as men take more responsibility with the child with special needs. Sometimes it seems that the women can't let go of doing all of the work and being overwhelmed all of the time. Let's get more organized and distribute the work.
5. We need more strength and stability in our marriage. It would help if they told us what we are doing right so that we could feel more secure in the relationship.

How men feel:

1. Men have an extremely hard time with all of the intense emotions involved with the child with special needs. They want women to be more rational and more supportive of their style of caring.
2. Men feel unappreciated for their efforts, especially for how hard they work to pay the increased medical bills and so forth.
3. Women are so intense that men feel like they're getting nagged all of the time.[25]

You may identify with a few or many of these statements. They may help you to realize you are normal in your thoughts and responses.

Avoiding Burnout

What can you use to cope with raising a disabled child?

When a child is diagnosed with learning disabilities, all of the attention is focused on helping him or her. However, you also need assistance in coping with your own feelings and frustrations.

Expectations lie at the root of burnout. When expectations about parenting are not met, your first thought is, *What did I do wrong?* Therefore, it's important to learn how to develop realistic expectations and how to recognize when negative self-talk defeats effective coping.

You can identify your own self-defeating assumptions and think of alternative messages. Be kind to yourself and accept yourself and your child as fallible. Parents cope better when they use personal strengths and talents.

Your life is changed because of your child, but it's not over. Scripture tells us, "My mind and my body may grow weak, but God is my strength; he is all I ever need," (Ps. 73:26, *GNB*). This verse may be of comfort to you, as it was to us.

We have learned so much over the years. Perhaps some of it can best be summed up in this statement written years ago by a brother in Christ:

> The disabled are the sign that all men have significance beyond what they can be, and do for us. To see the disabled honestly is to remind us that we cannot earn significance for our lives, it is a gift of God. Christ makes it possible for us to love our disabled brothers in a way radically different from the possessive love that thrives on the need to be needed. To love the weak in Christ is to dare to be free and to be free from dependency on their needs. God wants us to see each other as significant only as we exist in Him. We are each God's gift to the other.[26]

8

The Child Who Disappears

Just as parents can lose a child through death or disability, they can also lose a child in several other devastating ways: lifestyle choices, mental health issues, parental divorce, runaway or abduction losses, and more. Unfortunately, there is usually not much support given to parents who suffer these losses.

Perhaps one or more of these situations has happened to you. Maybe this chapter doesn't pertain to you at all, but you do know someone who would benefit from this information. Either way, read this chapter to gain insight on these types of parent-child situations that involve multiple losses.

Just Imagine . . .

Your first grandchild! You've waited for this day for years. And the parents, your son and his spouse, need you to help raise your grandchild for several years because of their work schedule. You invest yourself almost daily in this little boy. Then your son and daughter-in-law divorce. Daily interaction with this beloved grandchild diminishes to once or twice a month. And when he is 10, he and his mother move 3,000 miles away. Contact is minimal—no phone calls or letters. He exists in your heart and mind; but for all other purposes, he has disappeared from your life and your son's life. You visited him once, when he was 18, but that was all. It seems like a lifetime of losses for you and your son—for grandparent and parent alike.

Here's a second scenario of loss.

Just imagine: You've noticed that your 16-year-old has been acting differently for the past two weeks. She's not her usual outgoing, happy self. Her responses to you are minimal. One evening, she's especially distant, and you go to her room but it's empty. Many of her clothes and personal items are gone as well. There's no note. Just emptiness—she's run away, and your life has turned upside down and come to a halt.

And yet another scenario . . .

Just imagine: Your son has never given you a bit of grief. He's been compliant and very involved in your church. Others look up to him because of his Christian faith. In many ways, he's been a leader. Drugs or drinking have not been a part of his life. The son you've dreamed about having is reality. He marries and begins a family. Then your life changes. He rejects the values he's held all his life, leaves his wife and gets arrested for selling drugs. He's still in your life, but he's not the same child you thought he was. He's different, and he doesn't seem to have any desire to change. You're living with the loss of the child you used to have and probably will never have again.

These kinds of losses are every parent's worst nightmare. Your child is gone—missing for one reason or another. Some children purposely leave home to live on their own, because they want a lifestyle that is different from their parents'. Some are gone for other reasons. A child can become lost because:

- a parent has remarried and moved thousands of miles away
- a parent has remarried and wants nothing to do with their former spouse's family
- a child runs away
- a child blatantly disrespects your beliefs and values

The Lost Child

There are many ways in which parents can "lose" a child, as well as many ways for a child to become lost. One loss is referred to as an ambiguous loss. There is an incompleteness or uncertainty about it. And it's one of the most devastating because it isn't clear or complete. We all want certainty, even if the news is bad.

There are two basic kinds of ambiguous loss. One is when the family member is physically present in the family but psychologically gone or absent. We think of those who are older and have Alzheimer's or have suffered a stroke; but it could also be a child who suffers a mental illness or suffers a head injury and wakes up a different person.

The other type of ambiguous loss is when the person is still alive or present psychologically, but absent physically, such as a missing child. When this happens to a family, parents and others feel totally helpless. Parents become immobilized, having no way to solve the problem. The uncertainty leaves the entire family crippled. It's as though they are frozen in place.

And even though this loss may continue for years, they are denied the rituals we perform for a definite loss. How can you have a funeral or a memorial service when there is no death certificate?

Support and recognition for this loss are very minimal because others do not recognize it or they withdraw from it. One of the problems is that, unlike the death of a child, ambiguous loss may never allow you to move through the detachment that helps to bring closure.[1]

The confusion of ambiguous loss impedes the grieving process. It is one of the most stressful types of lost-child losses.

Runaways

Some children run away because of drug and alcohol abuse. When teens and preteens get involved in substance abuse, they may leave home to hide it from their parents. These are children who are using much more than their parents know or could imagine. They want to use even more drugs freely and openly, so they run away.

Feelings of failure can also cause children to leave home. Some run away because it's easier to live on their own than to live in a critical atmosphere.

Some children have left home because they were caught cheating in school or became pregnant and were afraid of their parents' disapproval.[2]

Let's return to ambiguous loss when a child disappears from home for one reason or another.

Loss When a Child Gets Taken

Why is child disappearance by abduction so prevalent today?

1. Predators. America as we know it has always been considered a safety zone. At first that was why so many people migrated to this country. But is it really? We never think that when we leave our children alone, going to school for example, someone is watching. When we leave them to play in the front yard, someone could be watching. When we leave them for a moment in the grocery store, someone may be watching. When we let them go to the mall, someone is watching. Why are predators watching us? It's easy for them. They look like the person next door. They go to work every day; they smile. They play with their dog, and our dog too. They're at church or in a neighborhood meeting. They're in the PTA. Predators are everywhere in our community. They are involved in everything we do, including walking and watching our children walk to school.

2. Many children are abducted by their noncustodial parent, or by another family member, such as an aunt, an uncle, a mother's boyfriend. Or the child may get taken by someone who has developed a relationship with the child and believes he or she is in love with the child. Then that person uses the child for whatever reason their needs may be.

3. The world we live in is no stranger to one of the biggest reasons many of our children disappear without a trace. Unfortunately, it's true that children are abducted and sold for body parts throughout the United States, Central America, South America and Europe. The Internet has become one of the greatest sources of business, and the organized underground business is one of the most successful businesses anywhere in the world.

4. Most of us don't even think of children used as pawns, but girls are kidnapped and sold for prostitution. This happens mostly in Asian and Middle Eastern countries.

5. Many children run away because their parent or legal guardian abuses, belittles or neglects them. They feel rejected with no one supportive to talk to, even at school.

Many children are placed into foster homes and then abused by their foster parents. When the child does report the abuse to Child Services, sometimes the social worker does nothing. Some social workers do not care, or are buried under a load of other cases.

6. Many parents drop their children off at school, drop them at the sidewalk and say, "I'll pick you up later" then never return.

7. Many men and women who cannot bear a child seek to adopt. The problem is that there are many illegal agencies that find and kidnap children for adoption or sale. The rewards in money and other compensations are great. Some kidnappers are hired to search for a particular type of child.

Fortunately, we have a support system in our country that works. We are very fortunate to have police departments that act within a reasonable amount of time when they get a call regarding a missing child. We are able to make police reports, and we have the recently developed Amber Alert system. Police can act on tips and leads to locate a missing child and continue to gather and build upon information to continue to do a better job at finding our missing children. The use of radio, television and newspapers gets the word out quickly when a child goes missing. Police may set up a command post near the missing child's home and use local volunteers, posters and community involvement to help find a missing child.

But just imagine living in a country that has no such system in place to locate a missing child. Many countries in Latin America are like this. When a child disappears, there is no one to look for them. There is no system in place—there is no Amber Alert; no national center for abused and abducted children; no Kid's Hotline; and no center for victims of violent crime. There are no organizations to assist you in conducting an investigation and to locate a missing child. In Latin America, you cannot pick up the phone and call your congressman, because there is none there for you.[3]

An encouraging development in the search for boys and girls who disappear in our country is the fact that more than 99 percent now return home alive.

The likelihood of finding an abducted child has sharply increased in recent years due to technological advances in the way searches are conducted and a greater awareness that fast action saves lives.

But each year, approximately 800,000 children are reported missing in America, including some who are lost, injured, have run away from home or have been abducted, according to the National Center for Missing and Exploited Children, the nation's leading clearinghouse of information about missing children.

Of those who are abducted, 200,000 are taken by family members, typically during a custody battle, while 58,000 involve non-family members who are familiar to the child.[4]

One major change is how quickly authorities now respond to reports of missing children, understanding that time is of the essence. Regardless of who has abducted the child, every minute counts, as 94 percent of recovered children are found within 72 hours, including 47 percent found within three hours.[5]

Today, social media such as Twitter and Facebook, whose 900 million users can access Amber Alerts fan pages, are increasingly used by law enforcement to instantaneously share news of an abduction. That has brought new hope for those who are still searching for the thousands of missing children who are still unaccounted for.

An Unrecognized Impact of Child Abduction

One of the most common reasons why a child goes missing is abduction through divorce and parental dispute. In relation to child custody, there are times when one parent wants to relocate. When the divorced parents do not agree, one of them may take the child and go underground and may even change their name and occupation so that parent and child can completely drop off the face of the earth for a while, maybe even forever.

With this type of abduction, the family of the abductor usually knows where the child is. However, for one reason or another, often they do not want to come forward with the information.

Family abduction occurs all too often but lacks society's recognition of its devastating and long-term impact. The public's reaction to family abduction declares that the child is "fine." This is because he or she is with the other parent. They may believe the left-behind parent must have deserved to have the child removed or that the matter is "only" a custody dispute between two battling parents.

The public's view of truly abducted children is defined by "stranger" abductions like Adam Walsh's (kidnapped and murdered in 1981; his father became an advocate for child victims and launched the long-running television program *America's Most Wanted*); like Polly Klaas's (kidnapped and murdered in 1993; her father went on to establish a foundation to promote child safety); like Amber Hagerman's (kidnapped and murdered in 1996; she became the namesake of the Amber Alert). But stanger abductions are not the most common occurrences. Evidence clearly shows that most missing children are taken by family members.

But why do family members take children? Is it for love? Most times, no. The typical motivation for family abduction is power, control and revenge. These characteristics are also prevalent in domestic violence cases. In fact, family abduction is really a form of family violence.

Some abductors may believe they are rescuing the child, but rarely do they resort to legal approaches for resolution. Some abductors are so narcissistic that they don't have the ability to view their children as separate entities from themselves. These abductors believe that since they hate the other parent, the child should as well.

Sometimes abductors feel disenfranchised and have a culturally different perspective regarding child-rearing and parenting. They may miss and want to return to their country of origin with the child. Perhaps you're seen some of the movies that describe this problem.

Child abduction victims are mostly between ages 2 and 11; about 75 percent are 6 years old or younger. Two-thirds of the cases involve one child. The most common times for the abduction, detention or concealment are January and August—coinciding with children's vacations and holidays.[6]

Most child development experts agree that personality is formed prior to the age of six. Therefore, the abduction of a young child will have significant influence on the person he or she becomes. It could be very traumatic. Significant people around the child will strongly influence his or her hopes, wishes, fears and attitudes. The abductor influences a child's attitude toward him or her, toward other people and the world in general.

Abducted children whose identities are changed may be told that the left-behind parent is dead or did not want them. Moving from place to place to avoid discovery, they are compelled to live like fugitives. They receive little or no medical care or schooling. These children are at risk. Our society's perception must be changed to recognize that the majority of family abduction victims live in dangerous and undesirable conditions. The losses and trauma can be overwhelming for them.

The impact on child victims will differ. Each child is an individual with different reactions to the circumstance and with different coping styles. The impact on a child will be affected by the pre-stressors in the child's life, the relationship the child has to the abductor, as well as the relationship the child had with the left-behind family and community. The child's age, character, how he or she was taken, length of time missing, what he or she was told, and his or her individual and cumulative experiences while abducted will also affect the child.

The left-behind family members, which include the parent(s), siblings, stepparents, step- and half siblings, grandparents, aunts, uncles, cousins and others, will suffer as well. Unfortunately, they don't receive the support and recognition they need. They live with ambiguous loss.

Initially, the left-behind family might experience shock and disbelief. They may have a rude awakening when the criminal justice response to a reported missing child is not all they might have expected. From their point of view, their child has been kidnapped. The family may have a support system or may consist only of a left-behind parent with little support to cope with the emotions of fear, grief and loss.

If the child is not returned quickly, the family is faced with a multitude of choices: Will they return to work? If not, how will they pay the bills? Should they hire a private investigator or psychic? Would that person be reliable? Could they get exploited? The family is emotionally distraught. They see their child's toys, clothing, room, playmates or a child in the grocery store—all reminders of their missing child and fear of the unknown. They wonder when, if ever, they will see their child again.

Convincing the authorities that the child might be in danger when taken by a family member is sometimes impossible and usually leads to more anger, much of it turned inward, which contributes to depression. Some parents engage in their own investigation, which can be dangerous. Others attempt to get publicity. Some people turn to a religious belief, while others feel abandoned and blame God for allowing their child's disappearance.

Some people react with physical symptoms, which include sleep and eating disorders, headache and stomachache. Many try to avoid their pain through the abuse of legal and illegal substances.

Time does not heal the wounds when the family remains in a state of limbo and is left with uncertainty of what has happened to their child. Today, we still hear about families who are searching for resolution to what happened to their loved ones considered missing in action in Vietnam, some 40 years ago, or in the Twin Towers in New York on 9/11.

Families need answers. Most searching families will, at some point, learn the fate of their abducted children, but the journey is grueling and often with no end in sight. Until the child's whereabouts are known and reunification has occurred, families cannot experience one of life's greatest gifts—joy. How can parents ever be joyful again when they don't know the well-being or the location of their child? Is the child dead or alive? Is he or she abused, hungry, cold, sick? There is no closure to their grief.

Time, unfortunately, provides additional triggers, reminders and pain: the child's birthday, the anniversary of the child's disappearance, each holiday. It can be an emotional roller coaster for the parent when "sightings" or "leads" don't materialize into an actual location and recovery.

Collateral Victims

The abducted child's siblings become forgotten victims. They have not only lost their brother or sister, but in many ways, they have lost their parent(s) too. Searching parents often put their focus and energy into finding the missing child and have little focus and energy left for the other children. Sometimes the siblings parent their parents.

These children experience conflicting emotions. On the one hand, they love and want their brother or sister to come back; on the other hand, they are angry and resentful of the attention their brother or sister receives in absentia.

Families of abducted children experience serious emotional distress. The siblings appear to be forgotten, and the family's history significantly influences how they handle this crisis.[7] The personality of young children who are abducted will be greatly impacted.

Most families live for the moment when they will be reunited with their children. When reunification occurs, certainly one nightmare will end, but it is not the end of the story.

The child may not want to have anything to do with the recovering parent or family. He or she may have been led to believe the recovering parent is a monster or is dead. Many abducted children have been taught to hate this parent. How upsetting! They have lived for this reunion day. Their lives have been placed on hold. They may have fantasized that they would all embrace and live happily ever after. The parent and family know and understand the pain they have endured, and they think the child might understand and have empathy. However, the child may feel very confused, angry and afraid. And the losses and grief continue.

After the Child Returns Home

After the reunification, it is best for the family to try to establish normalcy. Children will test boundaries. These boundaries should be established in a loving and caring manner to help children develop a sense of security. Most people who abduct children have difficulty with conventional boundaries and rules, so setting loving boundaries for the child who has come home might be difficult.

Recovering parents will probably wish to shower their child with gifts and fun times, but boundaries and limits should be set early on. If they are not, the child could become difficult and may grow uncontrollable. Also, the other children in the household, already resentful of the attention and gifts the recovered child is receiving, could feel there are double standards, and they may start acting out.

It is common to see regression in recovered children. They might go back to thumb-sucking, bed-wetting and baby talk. These kids may have some very special needs. Some have not attended school and will have difficulty being placed in the proper classroom or educational setting. Some were not allowed to play with other children and lack social and developmental skills.

These children will be sensitive to triggers and feel strong emotions. They may feel disloyal to the abducting parent, or resentful that their recovering parent did not come and get them right away. This type of victimization often leaves children with an inability to trust, which they may incorporate in relationships throughout their lives. As they grow and want to fit in with their peers, many children feel shame. They do not want others to know they were abducted children. They do not want to be looked at or made to feel different.[8]

Loss When a Child Chooses a Different Lifestyle

We lose our children in other ways. They're still a part of our life, but they've taken a different direction with their life, and many of our hopes and dreams for them and their future are lost. Often, we have to carry the burden of these losses by ourselves.

> My son is gay. He told me. Since then I've thought about the losses, not just for me, but also for him. It's true. I won't be going to his wedding or enjoying his children. And there are some conversations we won't be having either. Our father-son relationship will be different. I'm sad that he won't be part of God's normal plan for a male-female relationship and for what he will be missing. His cousins and siblings will miss out on him not having children. I'm sure there will be other losses I'll discover in the future as well. I'm just thankful for God's grace being sufficient.

Let's consider the losses that occur because of a change in your child's choice of values or lifestyle. You want them to take those words back and never hear them again. Sure, as a parent you've learned to expect the unexpected, but not something like this.

"Mom (or Dad), I'm gay" are perhaps some of the most painful words you could ever hear. The shock and feeling of disbelief bring your life to a halt. This is a time when, unfortunately, after the shock wears off, your emotions begin to fly apart. How you respond upon hearing the news can either draw your child toward you or shove him or her away.

Parents experience tremendous pressure when the announcement is made or the orientation is discovered. It can feel like your entire life has been crushed.

Keep in mind, this is not an offense against you. This is not something your child did to you. They did not choose gayness to rebel against you, to get back at you or to make your life miserable. In fact, it really has nothing to do with you. You did not cause this; it's not a failure on your part. Your expectations may lay shattered at your feet, but those are *your* expectations for your child.

This orientation is not news to your child. He or she likely did not tell you the first time he or she noticed a same-sex attraction. In fact, your child has probably lived with this for quite a long time. Your child had to discover how true it was. Do not ask if he is sure, if maybe he wants to take a little time and see what happens. Instead, consider the journey he has been through. Ask things like, "When did you know?" "How long have you felt this way?" and tell him how you are grateful he is including you, that he doesn't have to go through this alone anymore.

Your child was terrified to tell you. The risk he or she took is very real. Some gay teens have been shamed, banished, threatened, beaten and shunned by their parents. They know that once it is said, it cannot be unsaid. They took this chance either because they trusted you and hoped for the best, or because they could not stand to live inauthentically any longer.

Praying, wishing and believing will not make your child straight. If doing these things meant that homosexuality would not visit a Christian home, then we wouldn't see it cropping up so often.

Adult children are out of your hands. Even more than teens, adult children are beyond your parental authority. You have done your best as a parent, however flawed you were. (And we all were!) You must trust God with this child you have raised.

Put other peoples' responses aside. The opinions of your pastor, your Bible study group or your extended family are not as important as your son's or daughter's well-being. Put others' opinions aside and focus on how God would lead you specifically.

Finally, remember that we are not responsible to change people's behavior.

You have likely cycled through an entire catalog of extreme emotions: shock, disbelief, anger, guilt. Then came the questions for you and your spouse: Why did this happen? Where did we fail? And how do we as Christians and loving parents respond to our child's proclaimed homosexuality?

Stephen Arterburn, best-selling author and respected Christian psychologist, says that many parents of homosexual children withhold love and affection because they're afraid to appear approving of the gay lifestyle. The truth is that your child needs unconditional love and acceptance more than ever. Withholding love will only make a difficult situation worse. Remember that acceptance is not the same thing as approval. Acceptance means acknowledging what is true.[9]

Your sense of loss at this time intensifies if your child fully embraces the gay lifestyle. It's harder when you know that help and freedom from this are possible and available but your child rejects this option. For you, your child's choice is like a sentence of loss that has been given to you.

Remember, they control their behavior—not you. This is one of the hardest lessons for parents to learn.

When you talk, don't let your conversations be all negative. It doesn't help to lecture. Avoid legalism, by which I mean lecturing the child and telling him that he is wrong and you are right. Talk about their strengths; emphasize how we are all human.

Holidays can be difficult, especially if your child refuses to participate or wants to bring someone. If this happens, don't forsake the holidays, but spend them as they are intended. Do this for yourself and for your beliefs and peace.[10]

Many parents have described the grief they felt as the same as losing their child in death. The responses and reactions will vary but are quite similar. Don't be surprised if you feel confused and conflicted with what you're experiencing.[11]

You may experience some relief if you had suspicions. Perhaps others knew before you did. For some parents a burden is lifted.

Anger may come to the forefront in your grief. Perhaps you felt deceived by your child or blame your spouse for what he/she did or didn't do, or even yourself for not recognizing any indications. You will probably experience disappointment with your and others' reactions to the news, as well as your child. You could be angry at others for their open acceptance of this orientation.

Make a list of the various losses you think you will experience now because of this change in your child. You have expectations, and one may have been for grandchildren. What if your child experiences pain because of hostile reactions? You may begin living with fear over their safety, others' responses at work, prejudice, exclusions or a sexually transmitted disease.

Regrets and "If onlys" may begin to creep in and dominate your thoughts.

You will grieve for your child. You probably never expected this type of loss in your life.

There are two important things to keep in mind as you try to sort out your feelings. First, listen to your feelings. What you hear can contain clues that lead to a fuller discovery of God's will for you. Second, because some feelings can be confusing or conflicting, it is not necessary to act upon all of them. Acknowledging them may be sufficient, but it may also be necessary to talk about your feelings. Do not expect that all tensions can or will be resolved. The Christian life is a journey marked by perseverance and prayer. It is a path leading from where you are to where you know God is calling you.[12]

You have lost a dream that you had for your child. But you haven't lost your child. It's just that life for you and for your child is different.

Shattered Dreams

Every parent dreams about the future. The dreams may change from time to time as the parents become more aware of the unique qualities and characteristics of their child. But the dream remains, continuing to involve the best for their child. The dreams usually include the child developing talents to the fullest, reflecting the parents' Christian values, perhaps accomplishing what other parents' children are unable to, and thus fulfilling some of the unfilled dreams the parents had for themselves. But right now it may seem that those dreams are turning to dust, right before your eyes.

We use the term "prodigal." Not a pleasant term. It leaves a bad taste in your mouth and a sinking feeling in the pit of your stomach. It's a label given to people who are wasteful. But it's not just money they waste. It's the value system you've been trying to instill. It's their potential, their abilities, their health, perhaps even their lives. It's upsetting to you, but in many cases, they still don't care. When a child—whether a teen or an adult—becomes a prodigal, your dreams get tarnished. Sometimes they're not just damaged; they're shattered. Some are kept faintly alive like the smoldering coals of a fire; others die. It's difficult to say which is harder to take.

When a dream gets damaged or has died, it, like any other loss in life, must be grieved before you can move on. Some parents create greater pain for themselves by failing to say good-bye to a dead or damaged dream. They keep trying to resurrect their original dream. They attempt to breathe new life into it, like giving CPR to a corpse. When a dream cannot be fulfilled or is mortally wounded, the only alternative is to create new dreams. This is what parents who survive the years of their child's wandering have learned to do in order to survive, as well as to resurrect hope.

As willing as you may be to move on, the death of those dreams in which you have been so invested leaves you feeling abused and victimized. As one parent said, "I feel like I'm going through a divorce, not by my spouse, but by my 17-year-old. Our relationship has crumbled; he doesn't even talk to us anymore, let alone listen to any suggestions. And I've pretty well planned on burying all my hopes for him going to that Christian college. He won't go to church anymore. He told me that he doesn't even believe anymore. Maybe I ought to have a funeral service for his future!"

The author of *Surviving the Prodigal Years* describes the widespread impact of this child's behavior:

As the pain of the prodigal years increases, we find we are dealing with more than just our personal sense of guilt. As the load escalates, it sucks in other people. Both parents, whether they are currently married to each other or not, are snagged and flung into the angry sea of emotions. Siblings, the extended family, and friends are snared and left floundering, unrestrained for the shock of torn relationships.

The strain on the fabric of families can cause frayed edges and unraveled seams. We are so interwoven with one another that when one person rips away from the others, the continuity and strength of the family can be severely damaged.

We all react in our own way. Some withdraw; some turn to a friend; some become more united. People need to be extremely sensitive to the feelings, emotions and pain of the people around them. The prodigal years can cause parents and families to bond more tightly or to be ripped apart. . . . It can be easy to slip into depression, individually, as a couple, or even as a whole family. Having a prodigal child is very much like experiencing a death in the family. In fact, it is a type of death—the termination of family life as it was known.[13]

Rejection of Your Values

Having a child reject you and your values is difficult for any parent, but a different dynamic enters the picture when the child is an adult and you are older. The relationship has changed from parent-child to a more adult-to-adult connection. There is more of a peer-like relationship.

Of all child relationships, that of an adult child is possibly the most distressing and long lasting. With teenagers, you're always holding your breath, waiting for something to happen. But who expects a child of 30 or 40 to throw away his values and embrace those he formerly took a stand against.

When an adult child makes a major change in his life—such as leaving his spouse for another, proclaiming she's gay, getting arrested for embezzlement or involvement with drugs, becoming an alcoholic, or physically or sexually abusing his children, and so on—the hopes and dreams you considered reality get shattered.

You've already relaxed your role as parents. You were able to get your child through the perils of adolescence and have let your guard down. But then the news hits you. It's a crisis. It's a loss. And it's likely that you're now dealing with your own developmental losses as well. You may be seeing the top of your vocational ladder or be facing joblessness due to downscaling; you may be in the process of relocating, facing health problems or caring for aging parents; you may be starting to lose your contemporaries to death or illness, or may even have lost your spouse through death or divorce.

With everything else occurring in your life, difficulty with an adult child robs you of a major source of satisfaction. The way in which you talk about this child will change. Instead of volunteering information about her, you may be vague or hesitant to talk. If your child was well known or even famous, what you were known for has now been shattered, and some social status is gone.

If you were dependent upon your adult child in any way, you may feel torn between your need to stay dependent, if you're able to do so, and wonder whether or not it's all right.

Loss When a Child Chooses Substance Abuse

It's difficult to know how many families have been torn apart by just one child using drugs. When this is discovered, it's as though the entire existence of the family unit is focused on the child who is using. But everyone else has been impacted, and their lives have changed, probably not for the better. Every person, whether he or she realizes it or not, is experiencing some type of crisis as well as multiple losses. Perhaps you can relate to this mother's story:

I know our son started rebelling long before it imploded into disaster. We were losing him bit by bit as he pulled away from us, and he was living a life completely contradictory to the morals, values and Christian upbringing in which he was raised within our home. Unfortunately, he found an ally in a former female friend 20 years older. He began helping her with her son by staying in her home and watching him while she was at work. She led us to believe that he was helping her and she was helping him turn his life around and get help for the supposed depression he was in. At first we believed her, but then we saw the drugs robbing us of our son and turning him into someone we didn't know and, frankly, didn't like that much. And the drugs gave him a confidence that he could hide what he was doing, and when we were together he didn't realize that we saw right through him. My husband and I were working out a plan to take him away from the situation when we received a phone call from a bail bondsman letting us know that he had been arrested for burglary and he wanted to be bailed out. We didn't do it. We agreed that it was the safest place for him to be at that time. But we also had to call our own parents to let them know that he may be calling them and to please not bail him out.

And so the roller-coaster ride began. We discovered that grief and loss come in all different forms. The peace of our home was shattered when he came into our home and took my credit card and spent nearly $200 on drugs and clothes. He was so wasted that he blew off his court date and became a fugitive. My father had come out to go with me to his court date. I received a text from his friend telling me that he was hurting her. I discovered that night from her ex-husband that they were romantically linked, when I called him to get her address. I then called the police and sent them to the home they were staying in. I fled with my father and children and went back to my parents' house 60 miles away, at midnight. I didn't return until the next day when it was confirmed he was incarcerated and couldn't harm anyone.

Life for the next four months was a nightmare. Another robbery charge and drug possession were added to his list of crimes. We had to come to terms that he was living with and being supported by a mother, who had been my friend, and she was willing to give up her own children in hopes that he would marry her so they could carry on this Bonnie and Clyde, drug-addicted lifestyle. "Overwhelming" seemed like too tame a term for what we were going through. Many days I learned what the phrase "prostrate with grief" meant, and had it not been for my younger children, I may have sunk into a deep depression.

He had been bailed out, and after following through on two months of court appearances, they became homeless fugitives, not knowing where their next meal would come from. My husband and I learned what tough love meant. What parent's heart doesn't ache when their child calls and says he hasn't eaten for three days and he has no money? We knew we could feed him but not give him money or anything that could be returned to a store or sold for money. The drugs affected his personality and he became anxious when he needed to get high. His health was increasingly worsening and his anger continued to escalate. They took off together and we didn't hear from them very often. It was only out of desperation that they would call us and we would have to repeat that as fugitives we could not aid them in any way. If our son turned himself in we would support him for making the right decision.

There were many days that I didn't know if he was still alive or lost somewhere in the desert with nothing. She was finally convinced by her family to check herself into a rehab; and although she contacted us to let us know she would be leaving, she left our son on his own, sleeping in a sketchy motel without saying goodbye. He called us in a panic, and my husband got him to agree that he would turn himself in if my husband came out to get him after he had finished work that day. Our son was picked up by the police 30 minutes before my husband arrived to pick him up. My husband holds his emotions in quite well, but that night he cried the entire two-hour drive back home, grieving the losses that had been piling up as well as the time he was hoping to have that evening with our son. He had wanted to reassure him that we loved him and still trusted that God had good things for him in the future.

Our son is now serving a one-year sentence in a federally approved rehabilitation program. He is getting the help he refused a year ago and getting vocational training as well. We don't know what the future holds, but we are trusting God.

When the child who is using lives at home, you have still lost the child he or she once was. Your child has changed, and so have you; and so has the entire family unit.

Consider this description of child loss due to substance abuse:

It is an all too familiar story. A young teen who was once lovable, happy, a reasonably successful student and all-around good kid has become surly, disrespectful and defiant. He is wearing the uniform of the druggies, sweatshirt hood drawn up over his face, pants hanging low. He spends hours in his room, uncommunicative. He spends even more hours out of the house, places unknown. He is often sleepy and red-eyed when he finally does come home. Any request for information is met with hostility. When you've searched his room, you find drug-related paraphernalia and cryptic notes that are alarming. Old friends don't call any more. The kids he is bringing around have reputations for finding trouble. Now your kid has found them.

No attempts to talk to him have helped. You have begged, pleaded, cried, scolded and threatened. You have taken away privileges and things that are special to him. Maybe you've even had difficult talks with the school or the local police. Nothing seems to make an impression. You are watching your child disappear into the drug culture. The stakes are high. He's playing with criminal behavior that could get him in jail and he's putting things into his body that could kill him. You are right to be scared. You are right to fight for his life.[14]

Why do kids do this? Some begin to use because they can't figure out another way to fit in. The entrance requirements for the drug clique are easy. Just use and buy drugs.

Some kids get in over their heads and don't know how to get out.

Some kids who use drugs are self-medicating.

Some kids have the mistaken idea that in order to be okay they have to be better than other people. They know they can't compete with the "good kids" in the family or at school.

Some kids use drugs for all the attention it gets them. If he were the perfect child, would he get anywhere near the same amount of attention from you?

Some kids are just plain bored. Playing with criminal behavior is exciting.

Some kids think that using drugs is normal.

There is the possibility of true addiction.

In talking with families with a child who uses, they have described the losses they experienced this way:

- The loss of their dreams for this child
- The loss of the functioning of the family as one person is now missing in some way
- The loss of trust for this child since the child may resort to stealing to get money for drugs
- The loss of the feeling of safety for your belongings and other children
- The loss of physical and psychological health due to the stress of living with this problem
- The loss of prior family relationships since the child using drugs becomes the focus of attention
- Siblings may experience the loss of a prior close relationship with the one using drugs
- The loss of control or influence in the life of this child

Studies have indicated that there is an increased possibility that younger siblings will become involved in using drugs, thus compounding the losses and family problems.

Many families experience great stress, conflict and anxiety as a consequence of trying to protect the drug-using child from the dangers and life associated with drugs, and to limit the damage arising from their behavior toward the rest of the family. Parents and children often experience destructive disagreements over how best to respond to the child with the drug problem. The ongoing push and pull between whether to help, to what extent and in what ways usually is an enormous stress among family members.

If you have a child who is using, identify your losses and issues this situation has created. Don't try to handle the problem by yourself. Connect with other parents who have experienced this loss and let them help you. Drug use is rampant but so are the various drug education and intervention programs. Just look at the helpful resources on the Internet. Here are a few suggestions:

- Soberrecovery.com (a list of faith-based treatment centers)
- Helpguide.org (guidance in finding a recovery program)
- Recovery.org
- Drugabuse.com
- Family-inervention.com

As I reflect back on our family, we experienced some of these described losses when our daughter chose to go a different way for a time:

- Loss of trust
- Loss of security (he has been violent and stolen things from the family)
- Loss of the family closeness
- Loss of privacy (police show up randomly and have even opened the door to my home when I didn't answer right away)
- Financial losses
- Loss of physical touch—we can see him through a window but not physically touch him
- Dreams for the future are tainted—we pray that he will make the right choices, but jobs, romantic relationships and earning trust will not be easy
- Family losses—plans changing, witnessing parents (especially mom) on edge because of the situation, closeness with their brother—afraid of him

Other parents describe their experience of a prodigal child:

Our daughter has left home four times now. She came home again after being gone for several months. We talked for about an hour and a half and asked her to at least sleep on it. . . . She got up the next morning and told us she was moving back with her boyfriend. We pleaded with her to think about it and give it some time first. She admitted that her friends told her not to go back with him. She said he made her happy some of the time and bought her lots of things. My wife asked her if it was worth losing out on the family again. Our daughter said it was. So we have lost her again.

Our issue with our daughter was a matter of trust. That was my loss—a loss of trust in her. We are still experiencing that loss. But as I lost trust in her, I began to grow in my trust of the Lord. The first night she ran away, I came to the realization, "If you can't trust God when it's three o'clock in the morning and your 13-year-old daughter is missing, when can you trust

Him?" I decided there would never be a better time to start, so I went to bed and went to sleep.

One day I asked my daughter pointblank why she had left. I told her I didn't want to pry, but I also didn't want to make the same mistakes with the other three kids, and I wanted to try to understand. She still did not have much of an answer for me, except to say that now she knows it wasn't because of us, but it was something she had to do. At the time she was angry at us and felt that she had missed out on life because of her life as a PK. She also said that she knew the Lord was pinpointing areas in her life at the time, and she chose to run from the confrontation rather than listen with her heart and allow Him to bring direction and correction. She was searching for who she was and was afraid she'd never know if she stayed.

Our daughter knows that the way she left was wrong, that it brought pain on herself as well as her family. But she also knows that she had to make the journey one way or another. There were other ways to do it, but she knows that she had come to the place where she had to allow God to deal with her. Finding herself in God was the true test of this prodigal trip, and the price for that is beyond measure.

To others who are suffering the same loss, we would say, "Don't ever give up on God." His mercies are new every morning, and His grace is sufficient for all we need.

If I truly believe any part of Scripture, I have to believe Jeremiah 29:11, which tells me, "For I know the plans I have for you, plans to prosper you and not to harm you, plans to give you hope and a future." If this is true, God has a plan that I am unaware of—a plan for a future. If this is true, God has a plan that I am unaware of—a plan that will give me hope and a future. I am learning to trust Him a little more each day. And if this promise is for me, it is also for my daughter. I long for the day when her relationship will be restored to our Father in heaven.

A mother's 20-year-old adopted son started rebelling at 15—he was charged with robbery and spent time in a juvenile detention center. He thrived in that environment, became a leader in the weekly Bible study, was praised by the men who worked with him; but when he was released, he went right back to the old lifestyle and has been incarcerated on numerous occasions. He is now not speaking to her and blames his problems on her because she adopted him.

Her oldest daughter has been a strong Christian, and her mother has called her a "rock." A month ago, completely out of character, she left the state to meet a boy she had met on the Internet. And she is still not back.

Her youngest daughter has a speech disability, which has caused her to struggle in school. She is also adopted and, at age 15, became purposely pregnant. She had an early miscarriage and was devastated. She quickly became pregnant again, and at five months her amniotic sac ruptured. She was told that her baby would not survive and would die at birth. She was encouraged to get a medical abortion even though her baby's heartbeat was strong. She chose not to have an abortion, and a week later she went into labor and the baby died at birth.

This mother also had a miscarriage at five months eight years ago, and this has brought back all her hurt and pain.

These stories all reflect loss upon loss. Our children may still be with us, but who they were and who we wanted them to be has disappeared. Many parents have lost the child they wanted and dreamed of in this way.

When you hear words and see actions from your child that shake the very foundations of your home and family, everything you've worked for, prayed for and sacrificed crumbles.

You've become a hurting parent.

You hurt . . .

- because the children you love have turned toward self-destruction;
- because your children stand in grotesque defiance against you;
- because your mega-contribution to the lives of your kids is not being appreciated by them.

You hurt . . .

- because you feel like failures as parents;
- because you are haunted by your thoughts, *If only we had done this or done that;*

- because other parents—some with younger children or some fortunate enough not to have had severe problems with their teenagers—look at you like you are failures;
- because you are frustrated from going behind your kids, cleaning up their messes;
- because you have to mix with people at work, at community functions or at church who know about your children's problems;
- because you wonder if you ought to give up your positions at church or in the community.

You hurt . . .

- because you don't know for sure how to help your children;
- because you don't know what to do or how to think.[15]

You feel shattered when the dreams you've had for your child are destroyed. You want the best for them. You want them to be well adjusted and happy. You have hopes for their occupations, their spouses, their children, their accomplishments and their Christian life.

But sometimes the dreams have an extra dimension to them. You invest so deeply in them because some are really your own unfulfilled dreams or unbending expectations. I've talked with numerous parents who were living their lives through their children. What they couldn't experience or accomplish would be fulfilled vicariously through their children. There was no thought that it wouldn't happen; it was set in concrete, at least in the minds of the parents.

That is a dangerous approach. What happens when your child's free will and personal desires kick in and override your wishes?

Lost and Found: My Daughter

We've been where many parents have been. Our daughter chose a different path for several years—living with boyfriends, using cocaine and becoming dependent upon alcohol.

For five years, we felt as though we were in an emotional Death Valley. It was the most difficult time in our parent role since we placed Matthew in his home two years before. We seemed to go from one crisis to another during that period, experiencing situations that we had heard of in the lives of other families but had never anticipated occurring in our own.

Who would have thought that one of Sheryl's fiancés would turn out to be a drug dealer? We didn't, nor did she. Who would have thought we would receive a call from her to come and move her home because of a difficult situation with her female roommate who was dealing drugs? That was one time we felt more of a sense of control, because we were able to report the person to the authorities. But every day we lived under a cloud, and the losses never seemed to go away.

Despite the pain, we spent many enjoyable hours with our daughter that gave us hope for our relationship. But overall it was a time of sadness, because we saw no indication that she might reverse her course of action. We were often tempted to point out the pitfalls of what she was doing and correct her. Most of the time we kept quiet, however, because our mentioning the situation only aroused her defensiveness. And then we learned that she was already struggling under a load of guilt and certainly didn't need more. We prayed that God would bring others into her life who would share with her what we would, but she would listen to them when she wouldn't hear us. God did, and she heard them. After five years, Sheryl turned her life around. We were fortunate parents.

Grieve the Losses and Keep Hope Alive

Too often, parents carry the load of guilt and self-blame. Perhaps the more determined you are that your child will be a certain way, the more intense the pain.

It's normal to look at yourself and begin to blame. Yet even though we are all imperfect as parents (and some perhaps more than others!), the rebellion of your children doesn't mean you're a failure as a parent. My worth and your worth are not based on the choices our children make.

Who can explain why four children in a family have healthy attitudes and are morally responsible, but one rebels? We're dealing with birth order, personality differences, a non-Christian moral system in our society, and their own free will. If you are raising your children to be Christians and reflect that value system, you need to expect the possibility that any of your children may choose to stray from your intentions.

We need to wait with patience, which must come from the Lord. We'll suffer as we wait for our children and young adults to recognize their rebellion. But we must be there when they cry out for help and understanding. They may not use words to express their needs. Listen for that silent cry, and cry with them. We did. You may have to wait years before you hear it or see any sign that their hardness is softening.

When you reenter your child's life, do it slowly and with concern, not condemnation. Often your child knows the pain of guilt and conviction. He or she needs to know you are there not to rescue but simply to receive, love and help restore him or her.

Above all, keep the lines of communication open. Your letters and calls may go unanswered, but they won't go unseen or unheard. I worked recently with a parent, and over a period of weeks, six letters went unanswered. But the seventh one received an answer. Even when communication is strained or nonexistent, you can keep trying.

Never give up praying. Ask God for another person to enter your child's life and influence him in a godly direction. A peer or mentor can positively influence your child. He may reveal himself to others in a way he never can or will with his parents.

Grieve. Identify each loss and grieve them. Lean upon the Lord; learn to live on God's Word. Here is Scripture that is especially meaningful to meditate on every day:

Do not fret because of evil men
or be envious of those who do wrong;
for like the grass they will soon wither,
like green plants they will soon die away.
Trust in the LORD and do good;
dwell in the land and enjoy safe pasture.
Delight yourself in the LORD
and he will give you the desires of your heart.
Commit your way to the Lord;
trust in him and he will do this:

He will make your righteousness shine like the dawn,
the justice of your cause like the noonday sun.
Be still before the LORD
and wait patiently for him;
do not fret when men succeed in their ways,
when they carry out their wicked schemes (Ps. 37:1-7).

Your child may still be wandering. It may seem like it has been forever. And for some, it could be. Sometimes parents won't see the wandering child return. But never, ever give up hope. Keep praying. And perhaps for you, as it happened for us, the parable of the prodigal in Luke 15 will take on more significance. Actually, we can all relate to that story because in one way or another, aren't we all prodigals? It's just that some of us are more obvious about it than others.

RECOMMENDED READING

- H. Norman Wright, *Loving Your Rebellious Child* (Franklin, TN: Authentic Publishers, 2013). For more information and resources, see hnormanwright.com.

9

The Loss of a Child Through Trauma

It's especially difficult when you lose your child through trauma that changes the way he or she used to be. Your child is not gone. He or she is still with you but is not the same. Your child might remain this way into adulthood unless he or she receives help.

Sometimes as parents we wonder what is wrong, but we're not sure. In an earlier chapter, I described trauma, and perhaps you felt this was just something adults experience. Yet, parents can lose a child to trauma and not even be aware that he or she has been traumatized.

Children see or experience accidents. An adult lunchroom worker dies of a heart attack in the presence of the children. A playmate is seriously injured during a game. Any experience like this can create trauma. Unfortunately for many children, the event that created trauma in their lives may be at home. Physical, emotional and sexual abuse create lifelong traumatic results.

We used to say that in the United States few children experienced human-perpetrated disasters. The 1995 Oklahoma City bombing that killed 168 people and injured more than 680 people brought a new form of trauma to our nation; and then came the New York World Trade Center and Pentagon disasters of September 11, 2001.

Since then, we've experienced nationally traumatic events, such as the shootings in Aurora, Colorado; Sandy Hook, Connecticut; and the Boston Marathon. The repeated viewing of these cataclysmic events, especially the planes flying into the World Trade Center towers, and those shining skyscrapers cascading down in a smoky mass of destruction and death, have virtually tattooed those images on the minds of our children. At the time, *USA Today* told of a preschool child building towers out of Legos and then crashing toy planes into them again and again, saying, "They're dead. All the people are dead."

These are the traumatic events that draw national attention. But trauma of any kind turns the life of a child upside down. Some children experience it *directly*. It happens through accidents at school, attacks on our crime-ridden streets, or in the midst of secret, everyday violence at home. Other children experience trauma *vicariously*. With the media's constant replaying of mayhem and chaos, our wide-eyed children take on a new identity that is now described by a newly coined term for them: "living-room witnesses."

It is not a harmless phenomenon. To children, a trauma is a wound—an ongoing, festering sore that burns frightening messages into their souls:

- Your world is no longer safe.
- Your world is no longer kind.
- Your world is no longer predictable.
- Your world is no longer trustworthy.

It's difficult enough for adults to handle this, but children don't have an adult's mental or verbal ability or life experience to draw upon as they attempt to cope and find comfort. A child's mind doesn't work the same as an adult's. It is less sophisticated and processes information differently. The trauma brings into their lives a silence, an isolation, a feeling of helplessness. And there are warning signs that a child isn't doing well.

- He consistently doesn't want to go to school; his grades drop and do not recover.
- She loses all interest or pleasure in what she used to enjoy.
- He talks about hurting or killing himself.
- She hears or sees things others don't.
- He can't eat or sleep enough to remain healthy.[1]

Trauma is a condition characterized by the phrase "I just can't seem to get over it." And it's not just for those who've been through a war. I've observed it in a father who saw his daughter fatally crushed in an accident, and in women who were sexually abused as children or who experienced an abortion. I've seen it in the paramedic, the chaplain, the nurse, the survivor of a robbery or traffic accident or rape, and in those subjected to intense pressure or harassment in the workplace. And I saw it on the faces of those in New York on 9/11. I've seen it impact a class of fourth-graders when a classmate died in front of them.

The saddest thing is to see it in a child. All parents pray it won't happen in their family.

We pray to be spared because we know that trauma is much worse than a loss. Trauma is the response in any event that shatters your safe world so that it is no longer a place of refuge. And we know that children intrinsically need safety more than adults do.

Trauma makes us feel powerless. It's overwhelming for adults and life shattering for children. If we had the ability to see the brain of a preschool child after he experienced a trauma, what would we see?

Witnessing a tragic event is very painful. "Children often hold their hands over their hearts to show where it hurts most." And when they draw what they feel, "many . . . draw pictures of broken or blackened hearts."[2]

If your child has been traumatized, he may describe what happened over and over again to anyone who will listen.

A traumatized child may need to rebuild her entire world. Many feel their lives will never be the same. What used to be safe is no longer safe. When the traumatic incident stops, *it isn't over* for a child. A boy who lost his home in a fire said, "I don't feel like I did before. The fire burned me down inside just like it did the house."[3]

A child who has been traumatized by sexual abuse is likely to be abused again in the future. Unfortunately, this child tends to act in a way she believes will bring the abuse. She believes that more abuse is inevitable, so it's better to have some control over it when it occurs than to experience the stress of waiting for its arrival.[4]

The Effect of Trauma on a Child's Brain

One of the unfortunate results of childhood trauma is attachment deficit disorder. It's difficult for the child to emotionally bond with others. It's difficult for the child to respond to most social interactions. Some are inhibited or hypervigilant or ambivalent.

A child cannot learn when he isn't relaxed. If the trauma was recent, he could be living in a constant state of fear or anxiety. Your child may appear as though he's living in another world. He may also struggle with sudden mental pictures or memories of what happened; we call these intrusive thoughts and images.[5]

What's happening in his brain? His thinking process has been distorted. He will experience confusion, a distortion of time, difficulty solving problems, in figuring out what's best to do next.

As a result of trauma, something happens in the brain that affects the way we process information. It affects how a person interprets and stores the event she's experienced. In effect, it overrides her alarm system.

This will make more sense if you think of young children in their preschool years. Are they mature in any way? Their brains are especially immature. At a time of trauma, the child's brain tissue and chemistry are actually changed by sensitization. The child's brain is malleable, and it begins to organize itself around the experience of the trauma.

A child's brain responds to a trauma through imprinting. The more extensive and frequent the trauma, the more of an imprint it leaves. What is an imprint? It's like a processing template through which new information to the brain is processed. Think of this like a valley with a large river. When the rains come, it's fairly easy to predict what happens to the water. It flows in a predictable manner into creeks, then streams and then the river. But then a "100-year flood" occurs and the creeks and streams overflow their banks and cut new pathways for the overflow of water. The streams and perhaps even the river have been altered, and now they flow in different paths. And it tends to stay that way until another intense storm disrupts the flow. An imprint occurred.

Childhood trauma is the equivalent of a 100-year flood. Just as the storm changed the course of the river, so too trauma creates new imprints on the brain. Positive or neutral information from everyday experiences may be contaminated by the trauma imprint."[6]

It's difficult for a traumatized child to regulate himself. If he was abused, it's hard for him to understand what he feels and why he acts the way he does. Traumatized children often do things that don't make sense. Why does this happen? A traumatized child's brain is caught in a reactive cycle of perceived threats. And since his focus is constantly on threats, he lacks awareness of why he does what he does.[7]

Hypersensitivity can actually become wired into basic brain chemistry and bodily functions. Not only that, but after a trauma occurs, some of the attention and capacities in the brain, which were originally set aside for learning other skills, may be pushed aside from their original purposes to help defend against future traumas. In subtle ways the child's brain goes on alert. It's in a *preventive trauma* mode. And after enough chronic experiences, this arousal state becomes a *trait*. The child's brain organizes around the over-activated systems to make sure the child survives. Other skills are sacrificed by their defensive posture. It's not a pleasant way to live.[8] And many of our children are living that way.

The Effect of Trauma on the Body

What's happening in the child's body? Her body is out of sync. Her heart is probably pounding. She has nausea, cramps, sweating, headaches and even muffled hearing. Emotionally, she's riding a roller coaster and is irritable, afraid, anxious, frustrated and angry.

Since her alarm system is stuck, she's hyper-aroused. She could even suffer from high blood pressure, rapid heart rate or irregular heartbeat, slightly elevated temperature and constant anxiety. She may go through her life with her alarm button on alert, constantly on the watch for any possible threat.

How Trauma Affects a Child's Behavior

What's happening in his behavior? The bottom line is that if a child has experienced a trauma, whether an accident, death, divorce, abuse or whatever it might be, his parents ought to expect extremes of behavior—either over-responding or under-responding.

Either way, the child's behavior is off. She's probably slower in what she does, wanders aimlessly, is dejected, has difficulty remembering, and could be hysterical, out of control and hyper.[9]

With physical trauma, obviously some part of the body is impacted with such a powerful force that the body's natural protection, such as skin or bones, can't prevent the injury. The body's normal, natural healing capabilities can't mend the injury without some assistance.

Perhaps not as obvious is the emotional wounding of trauma. A child's emotions can be so assaulted that his beliefs about life, his will to grow, his spirit, his dignity and his sense of security are significantly damaged. He ends up feeling helpless. An adult can experience this to some degree in a crisis and still bounce back. However, in trauma, even an adult has difficulty bouncing back, because he'll experience a sense of unreality ("Is this really happening?") and depersonalization ("I don't know what I really stand for anymore"). So, trauma is indescribable, even for adults.

What Children in Trauma Need

How can you as a parent help your child at a time of trauma—both during and after? Children and adolescents have identified what they need, as well as what they *don't* need in a trauma or crisis. Here is what they've said works:

My mom or dad . . .

- allowed me to talk.
- allowed warmth and acceptance.
- listened well.
- respected my privacy.
- showed understanding.
- made helpful suggestions.
- was there when I needed him/her.

What doesn't work? When helping your child or adolescent, you would be wise to avoid these behaviors when interacting after a trauma:

Don't fall apart. Even though you are upset, stay together for your children. Falling apart tells a child or adolescent that you can't really be trusted with what they have shared with you. It's essential for you to stay in emotional control. If you know it's going to be a difficult day, or you're beginning to get shaky, hand off your responsibilities to someone else. Remember, you are to take care of your children. They probably aren't coping well, and they can't take care of you. Balance your reaction with empathy.

Don't speculate. Avoid sharing what you're not sure of or what isn't true. Just say, "I'm not sure, but I'll find out for you." It's a matter of trust. Don't say, "Everything will be all right" unless you are 100 percent sure you know what that means and that it really will be all right. False promises cripple your credibility.

Don't judge. Avoid any kind of judgment at this point, whether verbal or nonverbal. Focus on the needs of your child rather than on what you think *ought* to be or *should* have been.

Don't interrogate. You're not an inquisitor. Constant questioning can overwhelm and push your child or adolescent into silence. When questioning, be gentle and give her time to reflect on what you've asked.

Don't clam up. Even if you don't know what to do or say, don't withdraw. Children and adolescents need you around to support, normalize, and affirm them.

Don't overreact to anger. If children have experienced trauma, their anger may turn into rage or aggression. And these feelings can be confusing and frightening to everyone. It's hard for children to lose trust in people as well as lose the order and security of life. This deep fear spawns intense frustration.

Don't withdraw support. If children see others happily going on with their lives while their own lives are in shambles, resentment builds, and some of the people in their lives may respond as if nothing happened to them. Their experience and pain need to be acknowledged. Most individuals who have experienced a loss also experience a secondary loss when the cards and support stop coming. When this happens, they can't help but wonder if others have stopped caring, since the pain continues after the support stops.[10]

What Parents Can Do

Here's the flip side of the coin. You can respond in positive ways and offer practical help when your child needs it the most:

Do encourage emotion. Some of your child's angry expressions may not be acceptable, of course (you can't let him break all the windows in your house or burn down the back porch). But it's important not to overreact and cause your child to begin stifling his feelings. Here are some suggestions. A child can . . .

- talk it out.
- write it out.
- act it out in pantomime.
- sing it out.
- draw it.
- whisper it.
- count to 57 in sets of 3 and 4 (for example, 3, 7, 10, 14, 17— this takes some thought!).
- use exercise: running in place, hopping on one foot, hitting a tetherball, and so on.

If your child is shouting his anger at you, tell him you want to hear him, but it's easier for you to hear when he talks slower. Give him some guidelines:

- It's all right to feel angry.
- It's *not* all right to hit others.
- The goal is *controlled* release of anger.
- Ask, "Where is the anger in your body?"
- Ask, "What does anger look like on your face?"

Debra Whiting Alexander, author of *Children Changed by Trauma*, offers verbal prompts that parents can use to draw children out in conversation:

When there's been a crisis or trauma, it's important to help children feel free to speak their minds and to voluntarily tell you about their experiences of what happened. Never force or pressure them to tell you anything they are not yet willing to verbalize. Once they feel safe and comfortable, they may want to share with you what they went through. Here is a list of what you can say to support children who are ready to tell you their story.

[If you as the parent have also experienced this same event, someone else may be needed to talk with your child as well as with you. But someone needs to talk in this manner]:

- It's often helpful to talk about what happened.
- Talking about what happened can help you let go of painful thoughts and memories.
- Draw a picture of what's in your mind. Write a story about what's in your mind.
- Thoughts cannot make bad things happen or prevent them from happening.
- I can handle whatever you would like to tell me about. Your thoughts don't scare or worry me.
- Anything you think about is normal for what you have been through.
- How do you imagine you might think about this in the future? In one week; three months; five years; when you're a grown-up?
- Having frightening thoughts does not mean you are going crazy. What happened was crazy; you are not.
- The trauma is over. You have survived the pain it caused, and with time you will survive the memory.
- It's important to talk about what you're going through and what you've been through when you are ready.
- What is your understanding of what happened?
- What do you know about it?
- What do you want to know?
- What do you wonder about it?
- Where were you when it happened?
- What were you doing?
- How did you hear about it?
- Who was involved? Who else was there?
- What did you think about when it happened?

- What did you say to yourself?
- What do you remember seeing, hearing, smelling, touching and/or tasting?
- What most concerned you?
- What's your most painful moment or memory?
- What was your first reaction?
- What's not being talked about?
- Are other people right or wrong about what they're saying happened?
- What was handled well?
- Who was helpful and why?
- All of your thoughts before, during and after the event are normal.[11]

Do give them opportunities for creative expression. Children who have difficulty verbalizing their feelings may find it easier to express them on paper. Drawing helps kids gain control over their emotional pain and eventually eliminate it. When the loss is a death, drawing is especially important, because it allows children to actually see what their feelings look like. That helps give them a sense of understanding and control.

Writing or journaling also helps with children whose writing skills are developed. It's easier for kids to express on paper the reality of what's happened, along with their fantasies about it. Writing a letter to the deceased person—or even to God—can do wonders. Encourage your children to read aloud and discuss what they've written. But remember to respect their privacy; the choice needs to be theirs.

Encourage them to express their thoughts, fears and feelings creatively. For example:

- Draw a picture of your brother.
- Sing a song about Melissa.
- Write a letter to Dad, and ask Jesus to make sure he gets it.
- Write a book about Grandma.
- Tell Fido (or Dolly) about Justin.
- Help me remember what Fluffy looked like.
- Talk to God about Jimmy.

Do correct their myths. It's important to discover whether your children are practicing magical thinking. Younger children are particularly vulnerable to this. For instance, your child may have argued with a friend who three hours later was killed in a car accident. Now your child may feel responsible. One young girl told her dog to "drop dead"—and the next morning the dog did! She thought she made it happen. Identify and correct such myths as soon as possible.

Do allow your children to respond in their own way. Don't expect your kids to respond as you do. Initially, they may not seem upset or sad. Young children may even have difficulty remembering the deceased. You may need to help them remember their relationship with the deceased before they can resolve their grief. Showing photos or videos will help, as well as reminiscing about times spent together.

Do normalize the reactions. Keep in mind that a trauma can change a child's life forever. It's as though she gets on a roller coaster, but this one never stops. It's like having a nightmare when he's not asleep. And the experiences change from day to day. One day the event comes back in vivid color, the next day it's black-and-white, the next day she doesn't remember it and the next day she's numb. This all comes packaged with the fears that "I'll never be the same again," "What if it happens again?" and "I'll be left all alone."

What can you say to your children when they tell you their life has been ruined by what happened to them? You could respond with, "Yes, I can see where you would feel like that. I would too. But life is more than what happened. It's a part of it, and it feels really big right now, but it's not all of it. It's sad and even tragic, but this is not your whole life."

You can try drawing this word picture for your child: "Imagine holding a book, and your whole life is written on all the pages inside. Imagine that those pages of your life are filled with every experience you've ever had up to today. Now, where in this book would you find the scariest experience you've ever seen or heard about or been through? This one experience is one of the many pages of memories you've had in your life. Turn to this scary page and look at it, and now let's skip to a happier time in your life.

Tell me about this. You see, the scary experience (trauma) is not all of the book; it's just a portion."

The best approach you can take is to love, comfort and offer reassurance that you're there for your child. You normalize his or her reactions and feelings. Here's how you might say it:

I'm wondering if all your feelings are kind of confusing. That's normal. You're not going crazy. What *happened* was crazy.

You know, you're going to feel off balance for a while. It's like trying to stand on one foot. That's all right.

There's nothing wrong or weird or bad about your feeling this way. Any person—child or adult—would feel the same after something like this. It will be helpful to tell me what you need and how I can help.

Sometimes it's hard to talk about your feelings. We'll work together and find some easier ways to let them out.

Do encourage. What do children need most in a post-trauma situation? Many of them need to be encouraged just to be patient with themselves. And most of all, they need to know it's all right to feel and express feelings.

Do return to childhood. Attempt to return traumatized children to the world of childhood as soon as possible. They need the routine of school, recreation, bedtime, sports, church, clubs, parties, and the like. A child responds better when he regains the environment that gives him back the security of the routine. A child needs to be given permission to be a child again.[12]

If you don't see progress, don't hesitate to take your child to a skilled therapist who understands children's trauma. There is hope.

10

Choosing Family Balance

"My family died last week. What we knew as a family for the past 12 years is gone. It fragmented—fell apart. I thought I had just lost my son, but then it dawned on me. It was both—Ted and the family we had."

When a major loss invades your family, change is inevitable. Do you want to be a victim of the direction that changes take, or do you want to be in charge of it? You have a choice.

Strong words? Yes. True words? Yes. If you've already experienced this, you know what I'm saying. Some families draw closer and become more compassionate after a loss. Others become splintered and soon disintegrate.

We've seen them. When our son, Matthew, lived at Salem Christian Home, 20 children with multiple disabilities occupied his unit. Only a few of their families were intact. Most had fragmented.

Many families, instead of working out solutions for their pain and problems, will begin to attack each other in the months following a crisis, whether the crisis is the birth of a disabled child, the discovery of a child's disability, a death, or a child's rebellion. And if conflicts have been buried for years, the restraints are usually lifted at this time, and the conflicts erupt. So the family has to deal not only with the crisis itself, but also with the unresolved conflicts. Each drains energy needed for the other.

The Family System

Your family is a complex mechanism of various actions and reactions. Each person makes his or her contribution to the special mix that becomes uniquely your family. As a result, each family ends up with a personality all its own. Some call it a family system.

Like a ship sailing into heavy winds, that system sometimes gets tossed around, buffeted, even severely damaged. It flounders off course or loses its trim, especially when it sails headlong into devastating loss. Yet every family likes things to remain on an even keel. If a family is prepared and skillful, it can adjust to the threatening conditions. It can make the moves necessary to keep everything in balance, even as it is weathering the worst of times.

When Family Roles Change

When the body loses an arm (as when a family member dies), or when it is permanently injured (as in a disabled child), or when one part refuses to cooperate with the rest and does its own thing (as in a rebellious child), all the other parts are affected. They have to learn to adjust and, sometimes, assume new roles.

It is similar to an old-fashioned balance scale. If something is added to one side, it alters the other side by the same amount in the opposite direction. If the scale is ever to be balanced again, something has to be added to one side or subtracted from the other.

Your family is like that scale. The members have to adjust to handle the change and get back into balance. Many aspects of family life—including power, responsibilities and roles—may need to be reassigned. The longer the central individual was in the family or the greater the significance of his or her position (such as the oldest child rebelling), the more adjustments will have to be made.

I've seen cases in which one child committed serious offenses that drew attention away from the parents' marital problems. But when the child was jailed and no longer there, the problems became apparent, and another child began to be the troublemaker to ease the marital tensions. In some families, when a disabled child is placed in a permanent outside residence, other issues that had gone unnoticed begin to surface.

Between the time a loss occurs and the individual family members discover their new roles and stabilize, there's a time of uncertainty and turmoil. Because of the reality of the loss, it's difficult to make some of the necessary changes. Each family member needs time and space to deal with the loss in his or her own way. It may take awhile for each one to find his or her new role, especially following a death. You'll feel like a juggler at times, trying to deal with your own needs and still be helpful to the other family members.

After a crisis hits, you'll also have to weigh the needs of a particular family member against the needs of the family as a whole. You'll have to work for a balance.

What do people do who grow through their grief?

These families don't ignore the pain or try to circumnavigate it.

They don't try to forget the past or leave it behind.

They don't even "overcome" their grief, since it will always be a part of their life together.

Keeping Family Roles Flexible

How does a family keep the balance? We can observe some typical ways these families successfully navigate through grief to reach their new state of equilibrium. They realize that their members will take on differing roles. They also learn what to expect when it comes to family roles and responses in crisis. Most important, they're able to adopt survival attitudes based upon principles that have stood the test of time.

What keeps your family in balance? It's each person doing his or her part, pulling the load and contributing, because everybody has a role to play.

A family needs the support of individual members. If one person experiences a loss, crisis or trauma, there will be a change of balance. If a child fails a grade or is discovered using drugs, he won't respond as he usually does. Somebody in the family will have to pick up the slack in order to get the family back in balance.

If a family member dies, or is disabled and no longer does what he's supposed to do, this creates other losses within the family. If your child breaks his arm at school, this loss (of mobility, self-care, ability to play Little League baseball, do chores, do homework, practice the piano) impacts every other family member and disrupts the accustomed roles and routines. That is, other family members are recruited for his role and routines, which takes them away from their own routine and adds work to their lives. The family system has changed, individual responsibilities have changed, and relationships with one another have changed.

Healthy families know this will happen; they anticipate it, and they move forward with this new way of life for as long as it takes. More attention and help will now be given to the child with the broken arm. Tasks and chores will be reassigned to others. It's difficult, and there may be some complaining, but all of this has to happen to ensure that the family continues to function.

Has your family experienced this kind of transition yet? If not, you will in some way in the future. If a parent becomes ill and incapacitated, often a child or all the children have to fill in with some of the adult's roles. If roles aren't filled, the family functioning is thrown out of kilter. This often happens in a death, divorce or chronic illness.

It can all work quite well. The downside is that sometimes roles aren't assigned suitably, which creates serious consequences. What if a child is given a role that's inappropriate, such as expecting a daughter to take on her deceased sister's personality or asking an eight-year-old boy to be the man of the house now that his dad is gone?

Beware of such assignments. A new role can hold multiple gains—and severe losses.

The Role of Rules in an "Out of Balance" Family

Along with roles, every family has rules. Some are accepted and encouraged while others are rebelled against. For our purposes, the key question is this: What are the rules in your family about feelings? In some families, if a member continues with so-called unacceptable feelings, he or she may be rejected by other members. And so a split in the family system opens up.

Typically, some of the rules about feeling and acting are clearly stated while others are only implied. Either way, break them at your own risk! The following list shows some of the more common rules in dysfunctional families. Do you recognize any of them in your current family or your family of origin?

Here are some of the things parents often tell their children. These rules come through whether in spoken words or in the general atmosphere and ordering of family interactions:

- You must make me happy.
- Don't get excited (or angry, sad, fearful). Such emotions threaten to unblock my own tightly controlled feelings.
- Your job is to take care of me.
- You will be loved if you perform up to my standards.
- Walk on eggshells.
- Keep things orderly and calm around here.
- Live in denial.
- Don't speak the truth if it will make any of us feel bad.
- We must not openly grieve our dead loved ones; it's too painful for us.
- We must not touch one another; it could lead to problems.
- If you need something, I'll give it to you. I know your needs better than you do.

Which of these emotional responses do you experience? Which are a problem for you?

afraid	guilty	hurt
angry	frustrated	excited
confused	embarrassed	dejected
lonely	anxious	happy
sad	ashamed	elated
depressed	discouraged	isolated

Keep in mind that our children will probably express the very feelings we have never resolved in our own lives.

Remember that when we grieve, we may hold our emotional pain in our bodies in the form of muscle tension.

A healthy family, and one that recovers sooner, allows all its members to know, have and express their feelings in an appropriate manner. Instead of seeing this as a problem, they look at it as an opportunity for all of them to grow and to grow closer. Only in giving to one another and receiving from one another our truest and deepest feelings do we grow in intimacy.

Sometimes family members do indeed have the same feelings but express them at different times—even months apart. As one mother said, "It would have been so much easier if we had been in sync with our feelings. But each of the three children hit the anger stage at a different time. It was as though there was a balloon of anger floating through our home for months." It takes a toll on parents as they juggle their own feelings while they help a child process his or her feelings, which often change from day to day. You wake up in the morning after a day of anger expecting more of the same—only to find depression and quiet withdrawal.

Finding Family Balance After Loss

The goal is to reach a new state of balance in your family. If the rules are restrictive and burdensome, it becomes more difficult to do so. If the rules are aired and pared down to acceptable levels for all, then you can begin working on your new way of life together. You'll need to ask questions like these after your loss:

- Will we continue to participate in the same recreational activities? What new things will we do?
- Will we keep going to the same places we used to—or has the meaning changed too much?
- Will we still feel comfortable with our family and friends? What things can we do to help develop a new level of comfort?
- Will we find it difficult to fit in with other intact families? (Where does a family who lost a child fit in? Where does a family who lost a parent fit in? Now that the divorce is final, where are other divorced families we can connect with?)
- Will we stay in the same house, or will we need to downscale or move? What will help make these changes easier on us?

In regard to moving, one young father said, "We lost our home, and now we're renting. We can't invite our friends over. We're embarrassed, and so are the kids. And we can see it in the faces of others. They're not sure they want to be around us."[1]

It's easy for us parents to try to set the record straight so that every family member will respond to the missing family member in the same way. After all, it would be easier to handle a significant loss in the family if all the members were on the same page with their grief. But within a family, every person has his or her own history with the one who's no longer there. Others' perceptions of the person and their memories may be quite different from yours.

Sometimes others assume that each family member has lost the same relationship. This may not be true. They have not lost the same person—the person who was a certain way with and for them. It was a unique relationship for each one. And each family member might respond to this unique loss in a different way.

Instead of trying to set the record straight, try listening. Listening and reflecting may help your children sort out fact from fantasy—sort out the way he or she *wishes* it had been compared to the way it really was.

The point is, *you can't expect a child to respond the way you do*. But your child will learn from you by watching you grieve. This is another opportunity for you to teach your child about grief. Remember, in order to meet your child's needs, you need to take care of yourself and your child. Out of your strength (even in the midst of your own grief), you can assist your child.

You want to draw closer, but there is even a danger to all the closeness that occurs. It's supportive, but it could also make family members prone to blame or to get angry and impatient with each other. One may start blaming everything and everyone possible—except himself. This could be a child or even a parent. He feels the pain of the loss, but you don't see it. Here are some other possible responses:[2]

- A family member announces, "This isn't anything we should talk about again." She attempts to control everyone in the family by imposing a universal gag rule. She blocks others in their expressions of grief.
- Another says, "Of course you can talk about it—but not with me." Members in this family may grieve, but they end up doing it alone.
- Another may be responding to everyone who asks, "We are doing just fine, just fine, but thanks for asking." Yet the child and others may not be doing fine!

- Another may respond with anger: "This is just one more thing we have to deal with! Why do things like this always happen to this family?"
- Another responds with shallow platitudes: "Oh, let's not be sad about this. Our faith is all we need, and it's going to see us through." There is truth in this, but if sadness isn't allowed, the grief is buried, waiting to erupt someday. This is a form of denial.
- Another doesn't say much at all, but her body does all the talking for her. Her grief is absorbed into her body, and medical symptoms soon begin to appear—headaches, backaches, skin rashes, nervousness, indigestion.

Just imagine a child who has experienced a major loss and hears these various responses from his mother, father, older siblings and extended family members. What is he to believe about grief? How is he to act?

You can be the one to help him.

The Family that Survives Loss

How can families adjust to their losses—and survive? Each family is unique in its specific coping responses; however, we can identify some key characteristics of the surviving family. This top-seven list offers a quick summary:

1. Surviving families learn from others who've made it.
2. Surviving families express their emotions in healthy ways, recognizing that tears are a gift from God and don't need apology.
3. Surviving families don't blame one another.

None of us likes being out of control and left hanging. There has to be some closure to discover what created the problem in the first place. If we have an explanation for what happened, then we can understand it better, handle it better and feel relieved that someone else was at fault. The more serious the crisis, the greater we feel the need to discover the cause. Statements that start with

"If only you had, or hadn't . . ." or "Why didn't you, or why did you . . ." begin to fly from one person to another, and if a family member knows the other people's areas of vulnerability, the accusations can get vicious.

You may want to blame other members. Logically, blaming doesn't make sense. But good sense doesn't often prevail at this time. Rather, the surge of emotional turmoil and struggle for a reason for the difficulty become uppermost.

Because everyone is vulnerable at this time, accusations and other comments penetrate deep into the mind and heart of the receiver and will be remembered for years. No one wants to be unfairly accused or blamed. In the book of Proverbs, we read, "There are those who speak rashly like the piercing of a sword" (12:18, *AMP*), and "In a multitude of words transgression is not lacking" (10:19, *AMP*). These verses reflect clearly the pain of unfair accusations.

A better approach is to follow the guidance of these passages: "Pleasant words are as a honeycomb, sweet to the mind and healing to the body" (16:24, *AMP*), and "A word fitly spoken and in due season is like apples of gold in settings of silver" (25:11, *AMP*).

4. Surviving families look for solutions rather than create a war zone of blame. Surviving families don't magnify their problems, nor do they get stuck using victim phrases, such as these:

- I can't . . .
- That's a problem.
- I'll never . . .
- That's awful!
- Why is life this way?
- If only . . .
- Life is one big struggle.
- What will I do?

5. Surviving families don't allow themselves to become bitter; they refuse to live in the past or focus on the "unfairness."

6. Surviving families resolve their conflicts. New conflicts aren't automatically contaminated by a reservoir of past unresolved issues. (If a family hasn't learned to resolve conflicts *before* a crisis, it's not likely to do it *during* one.)
7. Surviving families cultivate a biblical attitude toward life.

In this survival list, each item is important. But I want to stress the final one, the one that should really go at the top of the list: cultivating a biblical attitude.

Over the years one passage in particular came alive as we depended on it more and more: "Consider it all joy, my brethren, when you encounter various trials, knowing that the testing [or trying] of your faith produces endurance" (Jas. 1:2-3, *NASB*). The *Amplified* version says, "But let endurance and steadfastness and patience have full play and do a thorough work, so that you may be [people] perfectly and fully developed [with no defects], lacking in nothing" (Jas. 1:4).

Learning to put that into practice is a process. And the passage does not say "respond this way immediately." You have to feel the pain and grief first, and then you'll be able to consider it all joy.

What does the word "consider" mean? As I studied in commentaries, I discovered that it refers to an internal attitude of the heart or mind that allows the trials and circumstances of life to affect us adversely or beneficially. Another way James 1:2 might be translated is this: "Make up your mind to regard adversity as something to welcome or be glad about."

You have the power to decide what your attitude will be. You can say about your loss, "That's terrible. Totally upsetting. That's the last thing I wanted for my life. Why did it have to happen now? Why me?"

The other way of considering the same difficulty, however, is to say, "It's not what I wanted or expected, but it's here. There are going to be some difficult times, but how can I make the best of them?" Don't ever deny the pain or hurt you might have to go through, but always ask, "What can I learn from it? How can I grow through this? How can I use it for God's glory?"

The verb tense used in the word "consider" indicates a decisiveness of action. It's not an attitude of resignation—"Well, I'll just give up. I'm stuck with the problem. That's the way life is." If you resign yourself, you will sit back and not do anything. But James 1:2 indicates that you will have to go against your natural inclination to see the trial as a negative. There will be some moments when you'll have to remind yourself, *I think there's a better way of responding to this. Lord, I really want You to help me see it from a different perspective.* Then your mind will shift to a more constructive response. But this often takes a lot of work on your part.

God created us with both the capacity and the freedom to determine how to respond to the unexpected incidents life brings our way. You may wish that a certain event had never occurred, but you can't change the facts.

One of the best ways to clarify our response to what we can't understand, explain or like is set forth in a phrase by Dr. Gerald Mann. He suggests that we are "free to determine what happens to what happens to us."[3] It's a choice.

Isn't that what Paul is saying in Philippians 4:12? "I know how to be abased and live humbly in straitened circumstances, and I know also how to enjoy plenty and live in abundance. I have learned in any and all circumstances, the secret of facing every situation, whether well-fed or going hungry, having a sufficiency and enough to spare or going without and being in want" (*AMP*). And his contentment came from the strength Christ gave him (see Phil. 4:13).

You and I have a choice—not about the difficulties of life, for they're inevitable, but about joy, for it's always an opinion!

John Killinger offers this helpful perspective on handling life's difficulties:

> Somehow, joy arises from loss and suffering and toil as much as it does from pleasure and ease. It is much deeper than the surface of existence; it has to do with the whole structure of life. It is the perfume of the rose that is crushed, the flash of color in the bird that is hit, the lump in the throat of the man who sees and knows, instinctively, that life is a many splendored thing.

Don't misunderstand me. I am not suggesting that God sends adversity to enhance our appreciation of life or to make us more aware of His nearness. Nor am I implying that the fullness of life comes only to those who have passed through deep waters, Rather, I am saying that God is present in all of life, including its tragedies. His presence transforms even these agonizing experiences into opportunities for worship.[4]

During the time of anguish as well as all the other times of life, our ability comes from our Lord. Take some time to meditate on these verses from God's Word:

Now to Him who is able to establish you according to my gospel and the preaching of Jesus Christ, according to the revelation of the mystery which has been kept secret for long ages past (Rom. 16:25, *NASB*).

Then he said to them, "Go, eat of the fat, drink of the sweet, and send portions to him who has nothing prepared; for this day is holy to our Lord. Do not be grieved, for the joy of the LORD is your strength" (Neh. 8:10, *NASB*).

And He will be the stability of your times, a wealth of salvation, wisdom and knowledge; the fear of the LORD is his treasure (Isa. 33:6, *NASB*).

11

Your Marriage Relationship

"Forest fire!" Those words elicit fear in the hearts of all who live in richly timbered areas. When a fire erupts, the best strategy is to confront it immediately and contain it with the appropriate equipment and manpower. Helicopters and planes drop fire retardant. And one of the first tasks is to construct firebreaks so that the fire doesn't spread. Sometimes those firebreaks work. But when they don't, the firefighters' efforts are taken away from the heart of the blaze to try to stop the new outbreak, and the time involved in quenching the fire gets extended.

A crisis with a child isn't much different than containing a forest fire. If it were your only difficulty, and it could be contained to just that, life would be easier. But what's happening with your child affects your marriage and your other children as well.

Not only does the death of a child change his or her parents forever, but it also permanently alters the couple's marriage. As individuals, parents must deal with their often confusing and painful thoughts, as well as their agonizing and overwhelming feelings. With the child's death, change is inevitable. As a couple, you must deal with how each of you has changed.

The Beginning of the End, or a New Beginning?

In a sense, you each have become something of a stranger to yourself and to each other. In the process, your marriage cannot be what it was before. It is the marriage of two people who have shared a very heavy loss, seen each other grieving and gone through the relationship struggles couples experience when a child dies. In one sense, the marriage relationship starts over as you both make sense of your loss.

You become new people, with no sense of whether you can or should return to being your old selves. You are likely to be beginners at dealing with the kind of grief parents feel and at coming to terms, as a couple, with whatever is going on in you as individuals. For quite a while, grief is likely to sap you and your partner of energy to solve problems, to talk about things, to think things through and to come to terms with what has happened. For weeks, months or even years, you may feel that you are in some kind of holding pattern, just trying to do the bare minimum to get along.

The death of a child remains one of the most stressful life events imaginable. One-fourth to one-third of parents who lose a child report that their marriage suffers strains that sometimes prove irreparable.[1]

Each spouse will go through a period of time when they are unable to give or receive needed attention. Both are so hurt that they can only focus upon themselves. Neglecting one another may take precedence over loving one another. This creates tension since each may expect the other to meet his or her needs. As one spouse said, "We couldn't help one another, and I didn't care how he felt since I hurt so bad . . . I just didn't care."[2]

The expectations you have of support coming from your spouse will probably not be met. In the early months, many couples find more support from other people than from their partner. It would be nice if you could find sufficient emotional strength from your spouse, but that may not be the case. Each of you is depleted, and your emotional resources are gone, so expecting your spouse to be thoughtful, giving, considerate and a good listener is not a reasonable expectation. Because of the intimacy of marriage, you're in the best position to support one another; but because of the severity of the loss, you're in the worst position to support one another.[3]

Over the past few decades, various reports on divorce after the death of a child show an increase in divorce, while others do not. When divorce does occur, it may not be because of the death. One writer said, "Marriages don't die with the death of a child, but often they receive an overdue burial." Divorce occurs because those who had already been having problems discover these problems are no longer worth trying to solve. After accepting the reality of the loss of the child, accepting the reality of the marital problems and the death of the marriage is a small step.[4]

It's been suggested that about one-third of parents lose their way and begin to drift rather than continue on their previous path. Some experience this temporarily, but for others it's permanent. Some feel there's no hope for restoring their marriage to what it was before. The life they had is no more. It stopped. Why? Usually it's unresolved grief. As I've heard many say, "When my child died, part of me died as well," and others added, "And so did my marriage."[5]

What happens to the marriage relationship? It will be taxed with extra strains and stresses. Some marriages break up over the birth and care of a disabled child or the death of a child. Why? Many factors contribute. But if the relationship was fragile to begin with, the difficulty with death or disability of a child could be the crushing blow.

There are a number of variables that will impact a marriage. Both mother and father are unique and bring their own history and past into their marriage. Are you aware of your spouse's losses over his/her lifetime and how well he/she handled those losses? If those losses are unresolved, their presence will be felt once again at this time. Ask your partner. Talk about this together. It's true that it may be difficult because of your own pain, but this is important for you individually as well as your marriage relationship.

Dr. Rosemarie Cook suggests that these additional variables will affect a marriage:

- the stability and strength of the individuals
- the maturity level of the individuals
- the strength of the relationship before the child was born

- the health, educational and financial circumstances of the couple
- the number, ages and gender of other children in the family
- the strength of the faith of the couple
- the social supports for the family
- the community services that will help care for the child[6]

Contributing Factors that Stress a Marriage

Let's consider the issues a couple may face. The first six months following the loss of a child is when the majority of divorces occur. Here are problems couples often encounter while dealing with grief:

- Lack of communication with one another, or not talking about significant issues, or the loss
- Disagreement on how to parent the other children
- Overprotection of the other children
- Difficulty deciding whether or not to have another baby and, if so, when
- Differences on how to grieve (one indication of marital difficulty is when a spouse judges how the other one grieves)
- Putting blame and guilt on self and/or the spouse
- Using alcohol and drugs to numb the pain
- Looking for someone or something to blame, which often leads to blaming the spouse
- One spouse wants to talk about the deceased child, but the other one doesn't, or they disagree on how much to talk about the child
- Disagreement on when, where and how to deal with a child's belongings
- Disagreement about whether or not counseling or a support group is needed
- Issues over finances
- Turning from one another and looking to others of the opposite sex for comfort

- One spouse may experience anger sooner or more intensely than the other, and each expresses anger differently
- One may tend to feel sadness sooner than the other, which is a difference in grieving
- One (the fixer) may want to *do* something to make things right again
- One may just want to *be*. Usually this person expresses emotions more frequently and more intensely
- Problems that were present before the child's death can become more difficult to deal with

"Why Do You Feel So Far Away?"

One factor affecting the relationship is emotional separation. After the discovery of a rebellious child's actions, or the diagnosis of a child with a disability, a couple is often so focused on the problem that they don't even share a cup of coffee or a meal. If they do sit down together, their discussion centers on the problem and rarely on themselves. When two people can't find comfort and emotional support from each other, they may find ways to numb their pain instead of working through it. Frequently, the substitute becomes another person or excessive involvement in outside activities.

It's ironic, but sometimes a close marital relationship can create additional stresses. The strength of the relationship can create vulnerability to the blame and anger those who grieve often displace on the ones who are nearest to them. And because of the closeness, you not only feel your own pain and grief, but also the pain of your spouse. The empathy so important in a quality marriage is now a conduit for more pain. This often makes it difficult to get any rest or relief. You may be fearful of asking for time out from the stress because of your concern for your partner.

When the grief is severe (as in the death of a child) or ongoing (as with a disabled or rebellious child), your security, strength, assertiveness, independence and health are all under attack. Normal differences and marital friction may get blown out of proportion because of the energy drain caused by preoccupation with the crisis. Here are some common problems that lead to marital distance:

- One partner keeps asking the other those unanswerable questions: Why? Why did this happen? Why us? Why did God let this happen? Why? Why? Why?
- One partner avoids talking with the other because of exhaustion, emotional distance or concern that it might make things worse for him or her.
- One partner makes irrational demands, such as asking the other to have answers, fix the problem or take away the pain.
- One partner makes rational but unrealistic demands, such as asking the other to do tasks for which the person is unsuited, or asking the other to take over the duties of both.

These and other communication problems will push couples further apart, which feeds an underlying, if not often admitted, fear of losing other family members (such as the spouse); any communication problems fuel that fear.[7]

"Why Can't I See You Grieve?"

We tend to assume that when there's a loss in the family, everyone grieves in the same way and at the same pace. That's far from the truth, for we all grieve in a personal way. Each person has suffered a different loss, since each person in the family had a unique relationship with the child. The different roles and relationships, as well as the amount of time spent with the child, will affect how one grieves.

As one wife said:

In the beginning, I was verbal and my husband was very quiet and to himself. He couldn't bear to see me so upset. He threatened to take Sid's pictures down if they were going to make me cry. It was very difficult. He didn't know how to deal with me. He tried to busy himself and not think. But Joe and I are closer now. It's hard for him to open up and now I can accept that. If we got through Sid's death, we can get through anything. —Patrice

A wife's open expression of grief often leaves her husband feeling helpless. Since he didn't know how to lessen the grief, he often makes attempts to lessen the crying. He becomes impatient with the seemingly interminable visible symptoms of grieving. In a rather futile attempt to calm the flood of feelings, Patrice's husband threatened to take down the pictures of their child, as if doing so would make her grief go away.

> Trying to figure out how to bring comfort to a grieving spouse is made that much more difficult by the fact that the mode of grieving changes within any individual from moment to moment.[8]

In the case of a stillborn or disabled newborn, the losses will affect more of your hopes and expectations. Seeing the football and the baseball glove purchased prior to birth now sitting in the disabled child's room, never to be used, may affect the athletic father more than the mother. If you waited for children until your mid-thirties and then had a Down syndrome baby, your hopes for other children may enter the world of loss. Or having one child for whom you held high hopes for academic achievement may become a major loss when he drops out of high school and then gets arrested for selling drugs.

Important Differences in Men's and Women's Grieving

You and your spouse won't grieve the same way, for men and women do it differently. A man will talk about the facts—"My son dropped out of school"—rather than his feelings—"I'm so disappointed with him. At times I just feel depressed and wonder if it was worth all the time and effort." After a while, a man becomes silent about his loss. His grief seems to decline more rapidly, which can lead his wife to feel he doesn't care as much about the problem or the child.

Let's consider these differences in more depth.

Generally, women tend to grieve more deeply, in an intense manner, and for longer periods of time. In her book *After the Death of a Child: Living with Loss Through the Years,* Ann Finkbeiner writes, "The mother takes the death harder, the father doesn't cry and doesn't talk, and the couple argues about the whole thing."

Women, by nature, often consider themselves the caretaker and tend to blame themselves when a child dies. *Why did I let him out of my sight?*

Mothers are usually more involved in the day-to-day intimacies with the child, so they have more reminders of their child's death, such as one fewer plate to set at the dinner table; when grocery shopping (going by the peanut butter, corn flakes, whatever their child's favorite and most hated foods were); the once-dreaded carpools that are now longed for; clothes shopping; and the list goes on and on.

Generally, men tend to focus more on tasks than relationships; they are defined more by their work than by emotional ties; hence, their grief becomes far more inward and less observable.

Men often see themselves as protectors and problem solvers. A man might regard death as an indictment against his ability to protect his family. *Why didn't I save him? Why can't I make my wife's pain go away?* The loss of a child can be especially devastating to the man who imagines himself in control. Following the death of an infant to SIDS, one man had this to say: "I run a company with thousands of employees, but at home I feel helpless."

Men generally receive less support than women during times of loss. One bereaved father claims coworkers constantly asked, "'How's the wife?' No one thought to ask how I was doing. Aren't I allowed to grieve?" In a society that pressures men to show strength during crisis, there's little wonder that many men cope through repression.[9]

Many men believe they should not cry; they are the family protector, they have to be strong for the family, so they suppress their grief. But women are allowed to cry while men are supposed to be strong.

Grief in men seems to decline much more rapidly than in women. In fact, grief in mothers after the death of a child tends to be particularly intense for about two years after the child's death. So, while the husband's grief is decreasing, his wife's grief is either increasing or at least remaining constant. This needs to be recognized and understood by both spouses as normal and has nothing to do with either parent's relationship with the child.

Wives tend to feel resentment at their husbands for seemingly being less tortured, while husbands have difficulty in truly comprehending the depth of their wife's mourning. Husbands may feel or think their wife is overreacting by crying all the time, and they are just not dealing with reality.

Most women deal with their feelings more directly in revealing what they feel (scared, sad, inadequate, and so on), and it is considered a statement of fact. They ask for support and consider it a practical response, not a defeat. Consequently, what a wife sees as an appropriate or helpful expression of feelings, her husband may see as a portrayal of a loss of control and/or a prelude to a breakdown for himself.

Men tend to grieve very privately. They cry, but they cry in private; they want to be alone to work it out in private, and wives would do well to let them have their space. Husbands feel a great pain when people ask how their wives are doing but never stop to inquire about them.[10]

Spouses won't be synchronized in their grief in the sense that when one is stabilized, the other will be down, and vice versa. Here are some other differences:

- *How you express feelings.* One may want to talk, while the other doesn't. If one tends to be talkative anyway, and the partner is quiet, the differences may be intensified at this time. Which feelings are expressed could also be an issue: One sheds tears of sorrow, while the other declares strong words of anger and protest. (Use the Ball of Grief at the end of chapter 3 to identify your feelings.)
- *How you face work and daily activities.* Often one person is immobilized by the crisis and the new set of responsibilities. But for the other, work and activities are a welcome relief.
- *How you relate to things that bring back memories.* Photographs and mementos of enjoyable times with a child who is now rebellious or has died may be a source of conflict. One wants them in constant view, while the other wants them out of sight. With a disabled child, one parent may still want to buy certain items, while the other sees no need for them.
- *How you react to the other children.* One parent may seek more involvement with the child, maintain a normal level

of involvement and share his grief, or the parent may withdraw to protect the child from his grief. Whichever direction one parent chooses, the other is likely doing something else. The problems here may multiply, because the child may want something entirely different from the parent.

- *How you seek support from others.* One may want to reach out to friends or a support group, while the other may not want any contact.
- *How you respond sexually to each other.* When a child dies, a sexual relationship can be affected for up to two years. Fear of having and losing another child and guilt over experiencing pleasure are common issues. To avoid further hurt, you may want to avoid intimacy. And often the one wanting sexual involvement has difficulty understanding why the other is avoiding it. This may be something that both need, but one cannot handle. The level of physical exhaustion and mental energy drain work against sexual interest.
- *How you respond to living your life as it used to be.* One wants to continue with life as it used to be because it helps to control the pain. But the other finds that carrying on the usual routine and socializing produce guilt. It feels like a betrayal. Sometimes with a rebellious child, one parent wants life to go on to let the child know that what he or she has done isn't going to get the family down.
- *How you respond to your Christian faith.* It can draw you together or become a wedge between you. Some learn to rely even more on the Lord and find the comfort promised by Scripture, but the spouse may feel that God has let the family down and want nothing to do with Him.[11]

Communicating When You Don't Feel Close

Have you ever felt like you're on a different page than your partner? Most of us have at one time or another. It often occurs during the grieving process. You would think a shared loss would bring you closer together, but often it doesn't, since you may grieve differently. You end up pulling away rather than sharing together.

Yes, you have lost the same child, but the loss for each of you is unique. There is nothing left inside and nothing to give, even to your spouse. You cannot seem to meet each other's needs or anyone else's needs. Grieving spouses are able sporadically to support each other, but they each feel a profound sense of isolation. Grieving spouses tend to focus on their own feelings, their own needs and their own day, which is normal, and they have little energy left to invest in others.[12]

Like everything else in your life that changes, so too does your relationship with your spouse. This loss is different

As we go through life, one or the other spouse experiences a loss or upset, but the partner is there to help. With the loss of a child, for any reason, you're both impacted at the same time. You're both in shock. You both come unraveled. It's like you've both been swept overboard into the ocean. You see that your partner needs to be rescued, and you want to, but you can't, since you need to be rescued as well. You want to help but you also want to be helped. When this doesn't happen, you may feel hurt and unloved and then angry.

You have both lost the same child, but your losses may not be the same. The mother-child bond is different from the father-child bond. You have lost your child, part of yourself and part of your partner.

How you grieve is affected by family patterns, personality differences, earlier losses, as well as your everyday life activities. Accept this difference and tell your spouse, "It's all right for you to grieve in the way you do, and I can learn from you." Have you ever done this?

To make sure to stay on the same page let one another know what you each need and do that often, for your moods and feelings are in flux. No one is a mind reader. Find the words you need to let your partner know what you are thinking and especially what you are feeling. You will feel less alone and so will your partner. It may be helpful to use the Ball of Grief in chapter 3 to help you identify your feelings. If either of you withdraw, it will generate confusion as well as rejection, which can lead to anger.

You, like others, may struggle with finding the words you need to comfort and support your partner. Sometimes the best thing to say is, "I wish I knew what to say right now to help you, but I'm not sure what to share."

"How Can We Reconnect Emotionally?"

Give your spouse the space he/she needs whenever he/she needs it. One day you may need closeness, and the next day you may need to be alone. Let one another know where you're at to avoid guesswork.

You cannot be everything to your spouse. You may be able to help in some ways but not others. You have your limits and so does your spouse. You will be limited by the differences in the way you grieve, your personality, mood swings, communicative differences, and so on. Some days you're depleted—running on empty. It could be that your spouse is too.

You can't do it all. There are times when you need to rely upon friends or a pastor or counselor. Several days after my son died, I was just drifting aimlessly around the house. Finally, my wife said, "You need to call Marv and go fishing." Part of me wanted to and part of me didn't, but I called. The next day I spent several hours fishing with him. I'm not sure how much we talked about my son, but the change and break from the grief were beneficial. I actually caught the largest trout I had ever caught in that lake. I felt safe with my friend.

It is very important that the people you choose to be with are safe and are good listeners. Grief support groups such as GriefShare can provide the support you need on a weekly basis (www.griefshare. org/findagroup).

"How Do We Stay Connected?"

To avoid these kinds of grief issues hindering their marriage relationship, couples can take several steps to minister to each other.

Set a regular time each day to talk about events and share your thoughts and feelings. Make it a private time, just for the two of you, and eliminate any possible interruptions before you begin.

When you listen to each other, hear what your spouse has difficulty putting into words. Reflect back what you think or feel your spouse could be experiencing. If your mate is struggling with some issue, don't attempt to fix it unless asked to do so. Listening is often enough assistance.

Agree on family activities that will always be shared by both spouses, even though you would rather the other person took sole responsibility. Agree also on activities that you each can do without relying on the other.

Make it a point to go on a date together each week, whether you feel like it or not. And when you do, put a gag rule on what you discuss. Concentrate on talking about issues other than the difficulty with your child. You need private time together to nurture your relationship.

No matter how strapped we were financially—and for a number of years things were very tight—we decided to never debate whether we had money for a baby-sitter for Matthew. Those dates were a survival necessity for us.

In addition to time together, each of you will need solitary time. Encourage one another to do this. Trade off so that one spouse shoulders the parenting for a while. One wife told me the 15 minutes a day her husband gave her as his gift were more than anything else he did (sometimes it was a half hour). Her husband even drew a bubble bath for her and placed her novel next to it to read. She said this daily ritual turned her into a new woman. Sometimes couples do trade-offs for each other for half a day each Saturday.[13]

"What About Physical Intimacy?"

You will probably be at different places in your desire for sex. One may want intimacy as a source of comfort and release, while the other isn't comfortable because of his or her emotional pain and questions about experiencing pleasure in light of their loss.

Men usually want to return more quickly to their sexual relationship, sometimes within a week, as they crave the comfort and escape from grief that sex provides. It tends to help them feel alive and pleasurable.[14]

To make love at this time means setting your grief aside for a time, and that is normal, healthy and necessary. Talk about your desires together. The physical relationship is a way to reconnect, and avoiding this may isolate the two of you even more than before.

If sexual desire is lacking at this time, it will return. Timing will vary from couple to couple.

Don't take it personally if your spouse isn't interested. If you had a positive physical relationship prior to the loss of your child, it may not take long to resume your intimacy. If there were difficulties, they could be intensified at this time.

Grief tends to leave many women sexually numbed, uninterested in sex and basically unable to respond. They may feel they should not engage in anything pleasurable when their child is dead. Many times they have a fear of pregnancy. After all, their husband was the procreator of the child who died. Their memories of sex that culminated in the birth of the child who is now dead cannot be reconciled with sex after the death of the child.[15]

The author of *The Worst Loss* said:

> In many areas of your life together, such as socializing, family activities, holiday observances, one of you will be readier to reengage than the other. If your partner wants to do something and you feel unready, you may need to push yourself. There is a balance to be struck in your effort. Your child and your loss will always be with you. But giving up your life with your partner and the pleasures you have had together will not make your loss less. Your balance has to do with holding on to your child yet finding a way to live your life, for yourself and with your partner.
>
> Your balance will not be arrived at quickly. Expect false starts and uncertainty. You need your partner's patience and your own. Let your partner know what you're feeling.[16]

Recommit to Support One Another

Here are some other steps that will strengthen your marriage.

Make a commitment as an individual and as a couple that "We will get through this together." Those who do this have a much better chance of having their marriage survive. These are the words of two individuals who made this choice:

> One thing we talked about the morning we found David dead was that we knew that people had problems with marriage after a child died. We made a decision that we were going to continue to be married and that we were going to have to work at it for the other two children. I didn't want David to be ashamed of us. We had to do

that for his memory too. I didn't want him to be the cause
of our marriage breaking up.—Erica

I can remember lying there that night and thinking that if
I could just go to sleep, and sleep for a year, things would
be better then. And I can remember that night, too, he and
I lying there and just making a vow to each other that it
would not tear us apart, because so many people, their family cannot survive. We held on tight and just decided that
we couldn't, we just couldn't let this destroy us.—Elaine

Have you made this commitment together? Those who have
supportive people around them are more likely to stay together.
Who are your support people?

Schedule time together each day—make this a priority. Have
you done this yet?

Another hurdle many couples face is being out in public and
enjoying their time together. Usually, one is ready to go out and
socialize before the other one is.

You may tend to feel people are watching you and expecting you
to feel morose since your child has died, and you should not laugh
again or have fun. So, go someplace where you do not see people
you know. You could go for a walk on the beach or to a restaurant
where the likelihood of running into someone you know is nil.
Usually, after breaking the barrier of going out, it becomes easier.[17]

*Recognize that neither you nor your spouse are yourselves; you're dif-
ferent. You are vulnerable and fragile, and neither of you will respond in
your typical way.* You will feel and act more irritable and may have
more conflicts. Have you encountered this yet? Have you talked
about this yet? Give yourself permission to be different.

Find other couples that have experienced similar losses, and
learn from their experience.

*Forgive rather than blame—there is a tendency to blame yourself as well
as your spouse.* It's easy to generate self-guilt, which is often unwar-
ranted and can become a barrier between couples.

Be open to counseling with a grief counselor or a group. If only one
of you wants to be involved, that's all right since it can still benefit
both of you.

Pray together and for one another. Be specific in how you would like your partner to pray for you. Read the Scriptures and devotional material together. Accept that each of you may be at different places spiritually. You're not in this experience of loss alone; God's guidance, strength and comfort can make the difference.

Consider creating a memorial for your child by planting a tree, building something practical at his or her school, by giving a scholarship, and so on.

Laugh—laugh together and look for the joy in life. Read books by Bob Phillips (Harvest House); watch films; play with kittens or puppies. Laughter is healing, and it is part of the grieving process.

In his book *The Courage to Laugh,* Allen Klein writes, "In the midst of death, life feels out of balance. Humor provides that balance by providing a fresh perspective and power in a powerless situation."[18]

12

The Other Children—
Your Response

After the loss of a child, if there are other children in your family—what do you say to them about the loss? What do you do? They're still with you, but your relationship with them has changed.

Children are not nearly as equipped as adults to handle loss, especially the loss of a family member. Their thinking processes are immature. They have few experiences from which to draw; they lack the vocabulary to describe their thoughts and feelings, and they take things literally. For instance, if you tell your kids that you have lost someone close to you, they may assume the person will be found again.

The younger the child, the more he or she grieves intermittently. Young children don't have an adult's capacity to tolerate the pain of a loss for a long time, so they mourn for a while, play for a while, mourn for a while, and so on.

Of course, you will tend to be more protective. It's a natural response. You're afraid of what might happen, so you may not want to let your remaining children out of your sight. (Many parents admit that they become overly strict and tend to hover.) You may feel like you're always on alert: "What if it happens again?"

When parents become overly protective, they do so for two reasons. One is to keep their children safe and the other is to protect themselves from any further pain. After a loss, most parents operate on the belief, "If it can happen once, it can happen again," rather than "Lightning doesn't strike in the same place twice." Whether they admit it or not, most parents are doing whatever they can to keep a calamity from happening.

Many children are aware of their parents' overly protective attitude, but some are not. Some children like the increase in protectiveness since it can help to rebuild their own sense of safety. Just as you create a "new normal" for your life, so too you create a new normal for your parenting style.

The challenge is twofold—helping your children rebuild a sense of safety while at the same time helping them learn through this experience and be more aware of some of the possible dangers in their world. If you as a parent are obviously hyper-vigilant or anxious, you could transfer that fear to your child.

One mother described the tension:

> You are sharing your child with your grief. There's no other way to do it. I'd love to turn a switch and go okay, this is the mommy that's not had this happen, this is the mommy who can have boundless energy, and isn't the world great, and you know. That's a fairytale . . . it's like you are learning to parent with this other thing in your life. It's always living with you. . . . It's REALLY HARD! Your energy level really is not as high as everyone else's, but people think because you've had a child die you'd be super, super patient with your children; you find actually you don't perhaps have as much patience as you perhaps should or did before. I had to struggle with this. This was a big thing to me. (Parent, four-year-old child died, three surviving children)[1]

Please Just Let Me Grieve

If you have other children, you are a juggler—you juggle between parenting and grieving—back and forth, back and forth. If you're the mother, you're more involved in this than your husband. Whether you work outside the home or not, you will be more involved. The demands of grieving and the demands of parenting will create a tension within you, and you, like many others, will wish that you were free to do one or the other. The cry is, "How can I be a grieving parent and a loving parent at the same time?!" One parent said, "I feel like I'm sharing my child with my grief!"

Another source of tension and discomfort comes from deciding the children's level of involvement with the funeral or memorial service. There's no rulebook for this, so it's a new experience for each grieving parent.

The juggling act is overwhelming for many, and some will decide, "I can do only one of these at a time. I can either grieve or I can parent." Some parents are not emotionally available to their children until their grieving has subsided.[2]

Perhaps you have struggled with how to put your grief on hold in order to parent your remaining child (children). One set of authors came up with the term "draining the tears," because so many mothers talk about escaping to the shower as a refuge. For many, the bathroom is one room in the home where they can lock the door and experience their pain and grief in isolation. The water sounds keep others from hearing their cries of pain. Some have done this grieving in the car while driving.[3]

Not only is there pain from losing your child, but also if you have other children, you are faced with how to be a parent to them. These children tend to get overlooked because you don't have much to give. You may struggle with their need for you to function as a parent when your desire is, "Let me alone so I can grieve!"

Here's what one mother said about her struggle:

> A lot of people say, "Well, thank goodness you have [a surviving child]; at least you have another child." Like, you've got one, so [deal with it]. There are some days when you don't necessarily think it is a blessing, because initially, you were so consumed with your grief." (Four-year-old child died, three surviving children)[4]

You may be aware that you're not doing what you want or need to do with your other children. Your grief drains your energy and depletes the emotional investment you want to put into them. You feel that you're not being the parent you want to be, which adds to your frustration and sense of failure. During the onset of the loss or crisis, remember this: It's unrealistic to think that you can act the way you want to with the other children. You just don't have enough to give.

There's Nothing Routine About Changing Routines

Family routines—traditions and daily routines—are difficult to maintain. What worked before doesn't seem to work anymore. Engaging in life the way it was before is just too painful. To survive, many parents change the routines. As one parent said, "We tried to function and do things that we had done before in the same way, but that didn't work, so then we tried doing them differently, and that didn't work either. So we started some new routines and schedules. This, too, is uncomfortable, but it seems to be working better."

> Having to parent a child while grieving helped me because it made me push forward. A child won't let you stop and do nothing . . . And I think if I had been left without him, I probably would have just wanted to pull the blankets over my head and stay there. . . . Once I was asleep, I just wanted to stay there. That was my escape. I just wanted to sleep. So, for me, it was a good thing that he pushed me to resume the role, because I probably would have crawled in bed or run away from it in that way. He kept me doing the usual things a mom does at home. . . . I think it helped me get back on track with life and start doing the things that most normal families do. (Two-year-old child died, one surviving child)[5]

In contrast to bereaved fathers, the mothers questioned now considered and evaluated how they responded prior to the death. Frequently, a new set of parenting priorities emerged. Mothers were determined to redefine relationships with their surviving children that would reflect these new priorities.

Here is what one mother said:

> I no longer get angry, because I can be very high-strung, and they [the surviving children] used to see me get upset if

something broke, something stupid, like a glass somebody gave them that was important. Now? Couldn't care less. Who cares? And I can see them seeing that in me.... I would never let anything, anything interfere with my relationship with them. My own personal family, there's been all kinds of issues that my parents would say, "Yeah, I would disown you because of that" or whatever; I would never, ever . . . They know because they've heard me say, "I would never disown you, I won't lose you. You could never say anything to me that's bad enough that I would say don't ever come back here to this house." That will never happen. (Anna, one-year-old child died, two surviving children)[6]

The changes in these mothers' parenting priorities ranged from no longer reacting to what they now perceived as the minutiae of life (tidy bedrooms, clothes put away, a broken glass) to a more fundamental shift in how they viewed parent-child relationships. This change was prompted by the loss that cast a shadow over all parental interactions with surviving children. Many mothers were concerned with avoiding confrontation and instead fostering unconditional acceptance and understanding. Attitudes and behaviors that had the potential to disrupt the relationship with their child were avoided at all costs.

Control and protectiveness were the central themes for bereaved parents as they continued to parent their surviving children, and it directly impacted their decisions and actions.[7]

You'll also fluctuate in your feelings and responses to your children. You may feel resentment that your other children are healthy or still living, don't seem to be as concerned or grieve enough, or they have adjusted too soon. Part of your response is your anger over the unfairness of what has happened. You may feel that you can't invest what you want to, or you've lost your ability to give. Or you may be afraid to invest because something bad could happen to these children. You could also overreact and overprotect. I raise all of these possible difficulties because just being aware of them may help you to avoid them to some degree.

When a child dies, parents are thrust into a multiple-crisis dilemma. Not only are they dealing with the loss of their child, but they're also struggling with how to offer care and comfort to the remaining children. In some cases they have to deal with the grief of their own parents, who have lost a precious grandchild. With all of these aspects to juggle, it's not unusual that the siblings have to cope on their own, since the parents just don't have the emotional strength to help them, at least not yet.

Can there be any emotional pain worse than the pain of losing one's child? Yet because of this, parents commonly shut down and respond in silence and secrecy regarding the child's death. This leaves the remaining children feeling haunted by their deceased sibling. They feel as if they must seal up their feelings, whether positive or negative, toward their lost sibling. If they had an enjoyable and close relationship, that bond must stay buried. If they had ongoing, unresolved conflicts, those, too, must stay buried. The children who remain after the death of a sibling often end up grieving alone.

Life for Surviving Siblings

The impact of the loss of a child on his or her siblings can vary. Many siblings feel ambivalent about the brother or sister who died and wonder if this somehow caused the death or could have prevented its occurrence. Some children even wonder if "the wrong child died." They think that perhaps if they had been the one to die, their parents might not be so unhappy. Some end up feeling unloved or ignored or overprotected or smothered. Some feel like they are different from other children.[8]

With a sibling gone, the roles and relationships with other family members often need to change. This, too, may entail more loss and stress. If your remaining child lived in the shadow of an older brother, he may now receive more attention and recognition for achievement but also have to be more responsible.

Your child who died fulfilled a specialized function within your family. Who will fill in for that missing brother or sister? Maybe your family role was tied into birth order. If your child who died was the oldest, your other child may have lost a caregiver or protector, or someone he or she looked up to.

Now there's a gap in the birth order. If there were only two, the remaining sibling is now an only child. If your child was a twin, it's normal for the remaining twin to feel that part of him or her died as well.

Siblings may share the same emotions parents feel (e.g., grief, anger, guilt), and some of these arise from fear and misunderstanding. If your child loss is from disability, siblings may be afraid they can "catch" the disability or may even have caused their sibling's disability by wishing Mom was not going to have a new baby or that the child would just go away.

Siblings may also feel jealous and left out as the child with the disability requires more attention for everyday needs. Other parents and sometimes siblings may be embarrassed about having a child or sibling with a disability; they may lash out at the child with the disability or illness in harmful, abusive ways for disrupting the family and adding stress to the family situation.

To avoid dealing with marital problems, some parents will turn most of their attention to the disabled child to avoid dealing with their spouse or other children. This can make things worse by creating an unhealthy bond between the parent(s) and child, taking the focus off their relationship with other family members and placing it on the child's illness or disability.

Guilt from Unfinished Business

There are other issues to consider. If you've lost an adult child, what if he or she and your other children were still caught up in sibling rivalry? This could feed guilt feelings as well as regrets in those who remain. Perhaps one or all of the remaining children will experience some relief that some of their lifelong hassles are now gone. These are normal thoughts and feelings. But they are more prone to feel uneasy for what they did not resolve with their sibling.

Guilt often comes to a child who loses a sibling, or to adult children, perhaps for different reasons. Guilt may begin with remembering how close they were when they were younger. Then they begin wishing they had done more to perpetuate that closeness but didn't, and now it's too late. Or maybe there were unresolved issues they now wish had been settled. Perhaps they wonder why their sibling died first, which activates survivor guilt. All of these feelings may be compounded by the additional loss of their not being included in decisions about the funeral arrangements, because all of that was left to the parents or to a surviving spouse and children.

There seem to be three main reasons why children experience guilt when they suffer a loss:

1. "She died (left or was disabled) because I did something wrong. I misbehaved!" Children have a knack for remembering things they've done that they think were wrong. They may have made a mistake, but end up with an incredible list of "if only" regrets.
2. "I wanted him dead. I thought it, and it happened." Young children believe they can actually make things happen by thinking them. It's easy for kids to think their anger or aggression killed their brother, for example, or made him the way he is. Because they take on this responsibility, they live in fear of being found out and punished.
3. "I didn't love her enough." Children believe that loving someone enough will keep the person from dying. They long for a second chance to make things right.

Anger at What Is

One other common grief response is anger. A number of beliefs trigger children's anger. They often feel abandoned and left to face life on their own. They're angry because their future has dramatically changed—they won't be with that special brother or sister anymore. I've seen younger children very angry with older siblings because of the chaos their rebellion created.[9]

All siblings disagree, fight and compete as children. What were the fights about? Were these fights always negative and harmful? Probably not. They had a purpose, a part of which was to educate and prepare children for life.

In the case of a child who is rebelling, the siblings could be struggling with disappointment and/or anger over the disruption of the family, grief over personal losses associated with a broken relationship with their sibling, or tension over conflicting loyalties to their parents and their sibling.

With a disabled sibling, the grief could be over the loss of the relationship they expected or the loss of routine in the household.

The Forgotten Griever

When a child dies, the siblings struggle with many factors in addition to their grief. They will live longer with the death than the parents will. They are now very aware that they, too, can die. Sometimes they struggle with guilt over their relationship with the deceased child and the parents' inability to prevent the death. Their emotional turmoil is a combination of their grief and their parents'. You need to be aware of any of their attempts to take away your pain by being perfect for you or trying to be a replacement.[10]

Your children's loss of a sibling is made even more painful because they're often a "forgotten griever." There are other names for those who have lost a sibling, such as the "lonely griever." There is no other loss in childhood or adulthood that seems to be so neglected as the death of a brother or a sister.

Tom was six and had two brothers—one was two years older, and one was two years younger. When his older brother died, he lost someone who had been a part of his life from the very beginning. In some ways, siblings define us. We become "Scott's brother" or "Mary's sister." It's common for a sibling to explain himself in relationship to a deceased sibling: "I act like my dad and John was more like mom."

Tom's future with his older brother was gone. No longer would they share the memories, family traditions or birthdays. A constant was gone from Tom's life. His brother's death made him feel older and much more mortal. His family of origin had shrunk by one-third. He found himself wondering if he, too, would die when he reached his brother's age. The bell that tolls for a sibling may keep on tolling with the message, "You're next."

When a sibling dies, very few take into account the depth of the bond that can occur between two siblings. It's as though the death of a sibling is dismissed, since a brother or sister is not considered one of the central characters of your life.

Why the silence? What are parents afraid to talk about? Usually it's blame, the shared feeling that they could have done something to prevent the death. Children, with their limited understanding and resources, wonder why they can't talk about it. They may conclude that their parents are angry at them and that the sibling's death is their own fault. This is especially true if the siblings didn't get along prior to the child's death. And so we end up with a situation in which the children *won't* talk because it would upset the parents. Everyone is busy protecting everyone else. But this kind of protection brings no healing.

If the child who died was the favorite, the parents may not allow the deceased child's name even to be mentioned, in an effort to prevent damaging comparisons with the other children. Most of us saw the perfect example of this in the heart-wrenching film *Ordinary People*. Buck was the firstborn who could do no wrong. He died while sailing with his younger brother, Conrad. After Buck died, the mother became cold and unloving toward Conrad, while the father maintained only a superficial relationship with him. Conrad soon discovered that he could never be what his brother was, and he struggled with his mother's comparison of the two boys.

Conrad lived in a home where his brother's memory was dominant, and his own hurts and angers were denied expression. His guilt intensified: He failed in school and eventually attempted to take his own life. He finally found the help he needed, not in his family, but in a psychiatrist who helped him unlock his feelings, face them and grieve in a healthy way.

Common Behavior of Surviving Siblings

When a sibling dies, it increases the surviving child's sense of vulnerability to death. His emotions run the gamut from being sad to being worried about who will care for him and watch over him to being pleased that he could be the center of attention now.

Fearful

Kids who experience the death of a sibling can experience a number of fears, including the following:

- Fear of losing parents, other sibling, or grandparents. They tend to see the remaining people as candidates for death.
- Fear of their own death, especially if they are younger than a sibling who died and they're approaching the age at which he or she died. If there was a disabling accident, they may become concerned as they approach that age.

- Fear of going to sleep because they equate sleep with death. Even the prayer "If I should die before I wake . . ." reinforces this misconception. Dreams and nightmares intensify the fear.
- Fear of separation because of the perceived insecurity of the home and family. They no longer feel protected but fear that anything could happen. And they're hesitant to talk about their feelings because they may upset other family members.

What does this jumble of feelings create in a child? Often it creates guilt and confusion. And a parent's response is so important. Parents may minimize their involvement with remaining children who need to be given the opportunity to express all of their feelings.

Unable to Grieve

Many factors may inhibit a child's ability to grieve the loss of a sibling. Here is a list of some of the most common obstacles:

- Parents have difficulty grieving past or current losses and have not provided a model.
- Parents are unable to handle their children's expressions of emotional pain.
- The children worry about how the parents are handling the loss and try to protect them.
- The children are overly concerned with maintaining control and feeling secure. They may be frightened or threatened by their grief. The feelings may seem too intense.
- The parents do not caringly stimulate and encourage the children to grieve.
- Surviving children may question their role in the death. Misplaced guilt is further enhanced if they have ambivalent feelings toward the deceased sibling.

Prone to Self-Blame

One of the crucial struggles for young children is reconciling what they know about death (for instance, it only happens to old people) with the death of a sibling or playmate close to their age. That's why so often a young child will talk about the "should haves." They may say again and again, "I should have . . ."

Help them finish the statement. It could be "I should have stopped him . . ." "I should have helped him . . ." "I should have told him . . ."

One mother found her son saying, "I should have . . ." over and over again. She asked, "I should have *what*?" He recounted a list of "should haves," all indicating that he should have protected his brother.

His mother said, "I understand, Danny. Daddy's got the 'should haves.' Mommy's got the 'should haves.' We all have them, and it's all right to have them. It's okay to know that all of us could have done something different and would have, if we had the choice."

Birth order once again seems to have some significance in how children handle these situations. Older children feel more guilt over having wished their younger sibling would disappear, while younger children feel more of a burden to replace the deceased child. Some adult siblings take it upon themselves to try to fill the hole in their parents' lives by constantly being available or even trying to emulate their dead siblings.

Resentful

Many siblings end up competing with the child who died, especially if their parents glorify the deceased child's abilities, intelligence or goodness. When the surviving children hear about their wonderful dead sibling, they may feel unloved or even jealous. They may feel it's an impossible task to compete with the memory of a dead sibling; this in turn leads to resentment, which leads to guilt.

Several other factors impact the lives of the surviving children. Consider, for example . . .

What was the intensity of the death? If a child actually sees a brother or sister die, it may bring on lasting trauma. Consider the impact of a child's discovering a sibling floating facedown in a swimming pool or seeing a sibling struck by a car.

What was the role of imagination? Even if the death occurred elsewhere, what actually happened to their sibling is left to their imagination. This could lead to denial of the loss.

What was the length of time in dying? When a sick child takes years to die, the other children feel helpless, abandoned and put on hold because parents have had little time to devote to their other children. These kids have also assumed many of the parental chores around the house.

What is the level of false guilt? The remaining children feel they could have done something to keep their brother or sister from dying. Many children thus live with guilt, self-blame and even the haunting question, "Why do I deserve to live and be here?" They also may feel that they somehow caused their sibling's death.

How to Help Your Surviving Children

What can you do to help your children? Give uninterrupted time to each child and listen to his or her concerns. It will also help you shift your focus from the crisis or problem to the normal affairs of life. We all need an occasional break from the crisis. Explain the situation as well as what to expect in the future to each child according to his or her level of understanding.

Regardless of the type of loss your family has experienced, the following steps will help your children through the process of grief:

- Children need to accept the loss, experience the pain and express their sorrow. Encourage them to talk about their feelings. Draw them out.
- Children require assistance to identify and express the wide range of feelings they're experiencing. Give them permission to cry and to feel sad and lonesome. Be a caring listener.
- In the case of death, children need encouragement to remember and review their relationship with their sibling. Looking at pictures and videos and recalling activities together are important.
- Children need help in learning to relinquish and say goodbye to what they have lost, whether it is a sibling who dies, or the death of their hopes, and their relationship with a disabled or rebelling sibling.

- Remember that each child responds differently to loss, depending on age and level of emotional maturity.

Perhaps the most helpful step you can take (although a difficult one because of what you're experiencing yourself) is to help your other children grieve and handle the loss from their perspective. They grieve as you do, but they'll manifest it differently. Too often, parents assume that their remaining children don't understand or are not that affected by the crisis; but that's not true. Fathers are especially prone to try to "rescue" the other children, but you can't protect your children from their own pain in a family crisis.

Amid all these painful situations and aching questions, there is much hope for the grieving family. Remember, no one can provide a quick cure for loss and grief. As a family, you must make your own unique pathway through the pain.

Your marriage and your other children don't have to be secondary casualties of the original crisis. You can take steps to strengthen your marriage and family life, and then you'll have a greater source of strength to draw from as you confront the issues facing you. As your family works, plays and worships together, you will discover a healing comfort in these relationships. Be sure you allow the other family members to minister to you as you minister to them.

13

Grandparents

"I expected to die first. After all, I'm older. Fourteen years ago, my oldest son died. I've recovered somewhat. But now, my grandson is gone."

It's unthinkable when a grandchild dies. It's an event that plunges a grandparent into the world of grief with no observable path to climb out. You are not only a grandparent but a parent who cannot protect your own child from the ache and pain of his or her intense loss of a child. It is a twofold sorrow. You grieve for the loss and also for the child's place and purpose in the family system. The intensity of your grief will be based on how close your relationship was and how much direct contact you had with your grandchild.

Grandparents have a special place in a grandchild's life. There are many occasions when getting together is a highlight for both. Often, a grandparent is the one who helps a child understand family history and has an influence upon the child's identity. Grandparents often remember more and provide continuity in family traditions.

Grandparents are also important in the transmission of values, ideals and beliefs to grandchildren. Certain traits are transmitted by skipping a generation. Some research shows that grandmothers play an especially important role in their grandchildren's values development.

Many grandparents influence their grandchildren in their roles of mentor or teacher, nurturer, and even as a playmate. A special bond develops across the generations, intensifying the pain when a grandchild dies. The losses will accumulate as the days go by.

Grandmothers who raise their grandchildren reported more overall stress and parental distress than mothers. Indeed, most studies of grandparents raising grandchildren find negative effects for the grandparents' health when they lose a grandchild.

Grandparents have every right to grieve deeply.

Your Role as Caregiver

One of the concerns you may have is how to help your own child who has lost a child. You want to fix him or her and make it all better. Your child can't be fixed, because she isn't broken. She needs your love and support.

The way your child expresses his or her guilt may be different from your own and you need to respect the differences. It will not help your child to be told what he or she should or should not be feeling, should or should not be thinking or doing. But it *will* help if you can listen and empathize when he or she expresses feelings of anger, anxiety or despair. Emotional support at this time can be a great comfort. You need this as much as your child does. Remember, neither you nor your child will be responding in a normal fashion.

When your grandchild dies, you feel like you're standing by as both a participant and an observer. Have you ever heard the phrase "a grief out of sight"? It's a phrase to describe the tearing apart of the relationship between grandparent and grandchild—you can expect *not* to have the support your son or daughter will receive. This will hurt deeply since your anguish is twofold—over your grandchild and your child.

You will experience awkward moments when people ask, "How many grandchildren do you have?" and you hesitate before you answer. Many respond to this question by including the deceased child and stating that one of them is in heaven. Or someone might ask a specific question about that child, unaware of his or her death. You could say, "I'm sorry that you weren't told that _____ died on (date), and we're still traveling through the grieving process. Thank you for asking about him."

When you're at your child's home and visitors arrive, you may be ignored. Don't take offense at this, for it's not intentional. As one mother said:

> The most obvious place to ask questions and seek support would be from family and friends. Or so I thought. With dismay, I quickly learned that family and friends found my questions, and my need to talk about my grief, tedious and tiring. One of my close friends hung up the phone on me one day after indicating she did not wish to associate with me until I had "gotten over it." I wrote her a long letter including a passage from "Please Listen."
>
> Listen! All I asked was that you listen, not talk, or do— just hear me. . . .
>
> I asked her to "forgive me for being irritable, irrational, angry and weepy at times. I need your understanding, your patience and your presence. Please don't offer me advice on 'how' I should be grieving; judgments of 'where' I am in the process; or 'what to do' to 'speed up' the process, and when I should be finished. If you don't know what to say, listen! Then, I will know you care."
>
> Even my patient, kind and loving husband grew weary of my distress.[1]

The burden of grief you feel is like nothing else. It is unique. Your experience is a double devastation, for there is the loss of the grandchild, which you can do nothing about, and the pain of your own child's grief, which you also cannot fix. You used to be the one to face the major problems of adult life, but now the mantle has been passed to your child.

Some have told me they felt like they were just standing in the wings of a play, waiting for their role but not knowing what it was. You have many more years of life experience and wisdom than your child, but it doesn't seem to count at this time. "Hopeless" is the emotion many have described after the death of a grandchild.

A number of grandparents from Sandy Hook Elementary School in Newton, Connecticut, were interviewed by *AARP Magazine*. The grandparents didn't know how to respond to their own children who were drowning in grief. They found it difficult to deal with their own pain when their own child was fragmented by this tragedy. They struggle with what to say to them that would help them feel better. But there was nothing.[2]

What you are going through may be best explained like this:

This can be a very difficult time for you. Sorting out your own feelings of grief and trying to find ways to be supportive and helpful for your son or daughter can be confusing and overwhelming. Even though your child is an adult, your feelings of nurturing and caring have not changed and you may forgo working through your own grief as you focus on the grief of your child. You may have many confusing feelings, about yourself as well as your child. You may feel angry, cheated, frustrated, powerless, or overwhelmed. You may see changes in your child that make you feel alienated, unloved or intrusive when what you really want is to be helpful and supportive. Please remember that this is a very confusing time for your son or daughter, too. They may lash out at you as you attempt to help or make suggestions about such things as funeral arrangements, care of other children in the home, or ideas about ways to assist in the healing process. On the other hand, your son or daughter may simply withdraw from daily living, become unsupportive and deeply depressed by the loss of their child. It is not possible to predict how a person will respond to a loss such as this and your own child may become as a stranger in your life, compounding that loss you feel as a grandparent. There is no set of rules to follow that will simply help everyone to begin the journey of healing and find a "normal" life again.[3]

Even though you are older and "should" be able to cope, the journey of grief can still be overwhelming for you. The more you can learn about the process, the more it will lessen the pain, to some degree, and you won't feel that you're going crazy. It would increase your understanding of the road ahead to reread the first three chapters of this book. But for now, here are the basic phases of grief you will encounter.

Predictable Phases of Grief

Denial and Disbelief

You may still be in the initial phase of shock, numbness and disbelief. The death of any child or grandchild puts his or her loved ones into crisis. Your feelings can vacillate from feeling numb or dead to raging disbelief. Denial will come and go for you and your child, and the words, "No! This can't be true. It's not right. It's not fair. Noooo!" will come and go. You will feel panic and an overwhelming sense of numbness, as though life has stopped. And in some ways, it has.

You struggle with how to help, but it may be that it's just your presence and prayers that are needed. Don't try to correct what your child or the other grandchildren say, for they need to vent. And so do you. Let your feelings out. Your family needs you to just be there, as you will need others to be there for you as well.

> You need to be aware that you too have needs and need to remember that others in your life who love you want to help you in the same way you want to help your child. Just as you reach out to "be strong" and "hold up for the sake of your child." Realizing that you need support and that you are devastated and hurting is a positive step toward healing. You will also be a positive role model for your child in taking steps to ease your own pain.[4]

The Search for Answers

In time, your thoughts and feelings begin to shift. You move to the phase of searching and yearning. You yearn for the one who died as well as look for some reason for this loss. You and your son or daughter will replay what happened. A pattern of thinking that generates guilt begins to develop from questions surrounding "if only," "should have" or "could have" or "why didn't." This comes into play as you search for reasons or meaning.

You, as a grandparent, may struggle with the guilt of "we should have lived closer" or "we could have spent more time" or "We're older and they were so young. It should have been one of us." You search for reasons and sense for this loss. It's important to find support from others who have experienced the same kind of loss. Remember that your own child's grief will cause him or her to be erratic in his or her responses to you at this time. They will vacillate from reaching out to you and wanting help to withdrawing. Don't take offense, for this is their grief talking.

Waves of Intense Emotion

The third phase can be described in several words: "disorientation," "disorganization," "withdrawal" and "confusion." (For a more complete list, see p. 26.)

During this phase, your tendency to deny your feelings will probably be stronger than at any other time. One reason is that feelings now may become the ugliest and the most intense. One emotion triggers another. You may feel intense anger over this loss, which in some cases brings on guilt for having such feelings. Then you feel shame, and the pain from these varied responses makes the desire to repress very strong. If some of your feelings shock others, you may want to repress them even more.

Your thinking patterns at this time will reflect a certain amount of uncertainty and ambiguity. You just aren't sure what to think or do.

Behavior changes occur in everyone who was close to your grandchild. You may become overwhelmed by feelings of emptiness and hopelessness. There is a big hole in your life that nothing and no one can fill. Your routines will suffer and get interrupted. You may find yourself vacillating between performing tasks that need to be done and then reflecting and reminiscing upon how things used to be.

You may feel angry at having to face the loss of your grandchild. We try to protect ourselves from the emptiness loss brings in our attempt to restore that part of us. You may find yourself avoiding events where there are children the same age as your grandchild.

Don't be critical of what others say and do at this time, including yourself. Talk about your grandchild. Reminisce with your family. Let others know you want them to talk about your grandchild.

All of the various phases overlap and come and go, and this is to be expected. There is little that is constant, stable or predictable at this time in your life. Even when you're younger, the loss stays with you forever; and if you're older, you may tend to dwell upon it more and more.

Will Life Ever Get Better?

How long will your grief remain? Recent studies have indicated, contrary to what might be expected, that the grief of mothers may be more intense after two years. The ramifications of this phenomenon means that the anger for mothers may be more difficult after two years after death when most social support is withdrawn and their own husbands are suffering much less intensely.[5] Even after five years, the measures of intensity diminish to levels only slightly below those of the first two years, while fathers show a steady decrease in their intensity of grief after two and five years.[6] Mothers tend to have significantly higher levels of anger, guilt and social isolation. Many of these same characteristics probably exist for grandmothers as well.[7]

Eventually, and no one can tell you when with grief that can go on forever, you will come to a phase known as resolution and reorganization. You will see changes in yourself and/or your son or daughter that show that healing has begun. The symptoms of "the crazy feelings of grief" have subsided even though they will come and go. It's all right for this to happen and for joy to come into your life again.

The truth of Psalm 73:26 (*GNB*) will be yours: "My mind and my body may grow weak, but God is my strength; he is all I ever need." You can and will smile again. Joy and sorrow are not opposites or intermingled. You will be a different person. You will see life, yourself and God differently. You will have different priorities and perhaps a deeper spiritual understanding of life's meaning. You will carry with you the knowledge that death is a part of life, and the end of the earthly journey. All who are born to the earth make the journey; it is the length of that journey that remains a mystery.

Nothing can ever completely take away the pain of losing a grandchild. The void in your life will always be there. What will change, however, is the searing, numbing pain that is so much a part of your life for a while after the loss. You will be able to speak about your grandchild with a smile, go to familiar places and be comforted by happy memories rather than wounded by the knowledge that you will never visit that spot together again. You will find yourself reaching out to others as others reach out to you to assist you in your grief. You will become a comforter instead of the comforted. No one can say when or how long, but one day the world will seem brighter. You will feel the healing warmth of the sun on your back and feel that it is a good day to be alive. You will think of the grandchild you lost and count yourself blessed for that child's presence in your life, no matter how short that time was.[8]

Perhaps you are the fortunate person who, over the years, has learned about the meaning and process of grief. You may feel a bit torn asunder as you attempt to handle your grief and the grief of your child and his or her spouse. You will have the desire to heal their wounds, to protect them, give answers that will help, fix them, dry their tears and make everything right again. And you will eventually be able to do that.

You Will Be a Comfort to Others

How can you help them and take care of your own grief as well?

First, just by walking through the door. Saying, "I'm here," and then giving a hug are often enough.

Be sure to read the rest of this book so that you are well aware of the road as you travel on the journey of grief. You may end up being the person to help your own children understand this journey. Listen to them with your ears, your eyes and your heart.

Encourage your child and his or her spouse to talk, for to be heard is absolutely essential for bereaved parents. Being a good listener may be the greatest gift you can give them. And it may be the most difficult thing you ever do.[9]

Carefully consider the following bulleted statements as you listen to and offer comfort to those who are grieving:

- When I ask you to listen to me, and you start giving advice, you have not done what I asked.
- When I ask you to listen to me, and you begin to tell me why I shouldn't feel that way, you are trampling on my feelings.

- When I ask you to listen to me, and you feel you have to do something to solve my problem, you have failed me, strange as that may seem.
- Listen! All I asked was that you listen, not talk or do—just hear me.[10]

What you do to assist at this time will depend upon your relationship with your child and some of the present dynamics. Your child may want you there in person to help, or he or she may want you to help from a distance. Before you do anything, ask. Some grandparents help by cooking, cleaning, being a buffer between outsiders and their child; and if there are other grandchildren, they help by caring for them. Your child may make decisions you don't agree with, but the one who died was their child.

Whether intentionally or not, a grandparent functions as a role model in front of his or her grieving child. Your manner of mourning at the time of your grandchild's death and through the long years of bereavement to come may profoundly influence your child's method of grieving. You have the opportunity, in your sorrow, to show through your words and behavior that it is possible to survive such an injury. Sharing your feelings of confusion, and not having an answer for why this happened, can help promote understanding between you and your child and his or her spouse, and help assure that they are not alone in their daze.

You can convey that "doing well" does not mean keeping feelings inside; it does not mean not talking about the loss; it does not mean not crying. You can discuss and demonstrate that suppressed grief is unhealthy, both emotionally and physically.[11]

Remember that the way you grieve and process grief may be very different from your own child's and his or her spouse's. And if they've never seen you grieve, they may be surprised at your expressions as well. Keep in mind that this journey of grief will take years. Your emotions, and theirs, will be confusing at times.

Don't expect consistency in the way you or they express emotion. They want your company one minute and the next they may want to avoid and hibernate.

Some may not want to talk about the loss, while others may want to tell the world. Some share everything on Facebook, while others are much more private.

You may see tension in your children's marriage, and there could be multiple reasons for this. There could have been problems before the loss that you were unaware of, or it could simply be they each process grief in a different way. Or one understands grief and the other one doesn't.

One of them may appear consumed by work, while the other can hardly function during the day.

They may have difficulty being around other parents who have a child of the same age as the one they lost.

The author of *A Grandparent's Sorrow* wrote:

Playing the role of parent to a grieving adult child will be both a blessing and a curse as you try to figure out how you can be most helpful in any situation. Because you will be eager to do the right thing, and fearful of doing harm, you may find that you are often timid in your responses. You will experience moments of affectionate caring and times of bittersweet emotional pain.

It is tempting for us to want to live in this world without having to suffer. And certainly that is what we desire for our children. We would like to protect our children from having to experience the distress that we have encountered. I have heard mothers say they would gladly go through labor for their daughter if they could, so that their daughter would not have to experience the pain of labor. Such is the desire to protect the child from what the mother feels as the harshness or unfairness of life. But even if such protection were possible, it would deny to your daughter the gifts that are abundant in the experience of *giving birth to themselves* as they give birth to their children. The same is true with the experience of a deep loss, such as losing a baby. We would like to believe that if we don't talk about the loss, minimize it, or even deny any significant impact, then we won't have to deal with the emotional problems that it presents. But truly it is a willingness to be drawn to the depth of despair that will allow our children to grow and mature emotionally and spiritually.

We try in vain to protect our children from the agony of death and grief. A wise parent, however, learns to trust the child's ability to swim in the sea of grief without drowning. That same parent knows that the child can only become fully alive by being submerged in the depths of his or her own sorrow, by experiencing the death and hell that is a part of grief, and finally by being restored to life as one forever changed.[12]

Perhaps you can relate to the words of this grandparent:

Many people assured me that I "would grow" from my grief experience. I was not interested in growth. Only years later, after much study and living through my grief, am I willing to accede to the possibility that grief holds the potential for enrichment and sensitivity. I finally can appreciate the following, printed in a grief seminar brochure.

> Grief and mourning can become:
> a stagnant pond—or a river
> a cave—or a tunnel
> a place—or a journey.[13]

Another grandmother wrote:

Converting my pond to a river, dark cave to a tunnel, and sorrow to a journey has not occurred in a linear fashion. My mourning continues to be an ongoing and uneven struggle. Particularly in the early years, brief glimmers of optimism were eclipsed by despair and depression. Anger usually overruled logic. Irritation displaced peace. I wandered between shock, depression, anger, irritation and, often, total fatigue.

When feeling totally bereft, I doubted my intuitive belief that I could survive. My training and experience as a nurse has taught me the need to heed and endure my chaotic feelings. But making choices on how to deal with those feelings often seemed beyond my immediate strength, and ability. Attempts to be patient with myself were not always successful.[14]

Will you continue to struggle like these grandparents? Yes, we all do.

Surviving the Pain of Guilt

In the journey of grief, guilt is a frequent but uninvited visitor that often tends to become a permanent resident. Logical, it isn't; but it gains a foothold anyway, for your feelings tend to override your logic. I've talked with grandparents who struggle with survivor's guilt. "Why should I still be alive after living all these years? He had his entire life ahead of him, and now he's gone, and what future do I have without him?"

Some struggle with their grandchild's death as some sort of punishment for something they did or didn't do. As irrational as it seems, as well as not being true biblically, the guilt flourishes. It's referred to as *moral guilt*.

Some experience guilt because of not living close to, or not being as available to, their child (the deceased grandchild's parent) as they could have been. Some refer to this as *geographic guilt*.

Perhaps the worst guilt of all comes when a grandparent is directly involved, in some way, in the death: perhaps the grandchild was in a car driven by a grandparent when there was an accident. It doesn't seem to matter who was really at fault; the grandparent still feels that in some way she could have prevented the death. One couple told me they couldn't be around swimming pools because their granddaughter fell into their pool and drowned 20 years before this. After 20 years, the guilt persisted.

Another type of guilt is what I call *moving-forward guilt*. It's when you begin to feel good or your grief begins to lift, but you wonder if this is all right, especially when your child hasn't moved forward. You wish you could fix your child and help him or her move forward, but you can't. Comparing your grief with others' doesn't work. Perhaps the other set of grandparents who lived so close to your grandchild are devastated, but you're not, since you didn't have the same history of contact and involvement.

If you struggle with guilt, write a letter to your guilt and ask it if it has any value. You could also list "Three good reasons to experience guilt." You see, guilt is one of the unproductive emotions you need to drive from your life. There is one solution for persistent guilt: It's called self-forgiveness. Self-forgiveness is a process that starts with asking God's forgiveness and then asking forgiveness of any others you believe you have wronged. While you're writing that letter to guilt, it may be helpful for you to write a letter of forgiveness to yourself.[15]

Other Types of Loss

There are other ways than death to experience the loss of a grand-child. When your children move across country or to another country, face-to-face visits are necessarily infrequent. The opportunity for contact has improved with communication technology such as FaceTime and Skype.

Other losses may be devastating, such as divorce and the other parent's custody of the children. Your child's ex-spouse decides when and where the children are available to you. You feel helpless.

A grandparent's intensity of grief and reports of symptoms of post-traumatic stress disorder were higher when loss of contact was related to family feud or divorce than when resulting from a geographic separation. What can you do? Allow yourself to grieve.

Practical Helps for Your Family

When it is loss through death, you could offer to help with the practical demands of family life, such as the care of other grandchildren who will be grieving and who may be feeling very left out. Looking after any family pets, or perhaps doing a little work around the home, could relieve some of the pressures on your daughter or son—especially if your child is a single parent. It's important to pace yourself so that you don't get overtired. You need to cope with your own grief and find time to replenish your energy. Otherwise, you'll have nothing to give.

If the relationship between you and your child has been difficult, it may not be easy to speak about your thoughts and fears.

If there are surviving grandchildren in the family, you may find that you are able to offer stability, comfort and support, especially while the normal patterns of family life are disrupted and disorganized. For both grandparents and grandchildren, this will be a significant time, and new bonds might well be forged that could last a lifetime. You and your grandchildren can gain great strength and companionship as you spend time with each other, sharing in activities, even if not talking about your grief directly.[16]

In the midst of companionship with your remaining grandchildren, you could be the one to help them with their grief. Just as grandparents are forgotten grievers, so too are children. Keep in mind that the grief of children is different from your own grief. Just like adults, each child may grieve differently. Children move in and out of grief, and for them it is a process. Many children do not complete their grieving until they become adults.

Alan Wolfelt, author of *A Child's View of Grief*, offers some practical guidelines:

- Don't lie or tell half-truths to children.
- Don't wait for one big tell-all to begin to help children understand death.
- Encourage children to ask questions about death.
- Don't assume that children always grieve in some kind of orderly and predictable way.
- Let children know that you really want to understand.
- Don't misunderstand children's grief process that may seem, to adults, like a lack of feelings.
- Allow children to participate in the funeral.
- Don't forget about the concept of magical thinking, that thoughts and words have the power to create illness, injury and death.
- Remember that feeling relief doesn't mean a lack of love.
- Realize that children's bodies react when they experience grief.
- Don't feel bad when you don't have all the answers for your grandchild about religion or death.
- Keep in mind that grief is complicated.[17]

Your grandchildren will probably mourn more through their behavior than by talking. Each child's response to death will be influenced by factors such as the type of relationship he or she had with the deceased brother or sister and how the sibling died—the cause, whether it was anticipated or sudden, traumatic, and so on. The chronological/developmental age of the child affects his or her grief and level of understanding. The uniqueness of each child's personality will be reflected in how he or she grieves. For example, a talkative, extroverted child will respond differently than a quiet, introverted child. The child's experience with loss and with previous death will have an impact as well. What a child has learned from previous losses will surface with the new loss.

Above all, stay in contact with your grandchildren. If you are not geographically near them, you can still stay in close contact by phone, email, text, FaceTime, Skype. Create an ongoing game that you play with them each time you talk. Teach them, by your example of expressing love and understanding of their grief journey, but also let them teach you.

Helping Others Help You

What about you? You will become a major source of comfort to your child and spouse and remaining grandchildren. But it's not all about what you do for others; it's also about what you need and what others can do for you. Many will not know what you need, so it may be helpful to make a copy of these guidelines, from Mary Lou Reed's book *Grandparents Cry Twice,* to give to others. These guidelines will help them know how to respond to you and understand the grieving process.

I am in grief and will probably experience this for a number of years.

I am not the same person I was, so please be patient with changes you see in me.

The two worst things that others can do is to avoid me or fail to mention my grandchild's name or talk about him/her.

I don't have the plague; and if you're uncomfortable around me or don't know what to say, just say so, for I understand.

It helps to know my grandchild _____ is not forgotten. His (her) name is so important. If you have memories or pictures, please share them with me.

When I cry in front of you, it's normal, and you don't have to do anything except just be there and be patient. My tears are a gift from God.

Instead of asking, "How are you?" it's better to ask me, "How are you really doing today?" or "How are you handling life today?" or "On a scale of 0 to 10, where are you today with your grief?"

When you see that I'm having a good day, don't assume that each day will be like this for me; the next day could be very difficult.

This is normal. Please do not try to fix me or change me, or my responses, or suggest drugs or other things to help me.

I would appreciate your listening to me, especially when I am struggling with answers to questions that may not have any answers.

Thank you for considering my request.[18]

Appendix

GriefShare—GriefShare is a friendly, caring group of people who will walk alongside you through one of life's most difficult experiences. You don't have to go through the grieving process alone. The GriefShare series can be ordered at hnormanwright.com, or go to griefshare.com and type in your zip code to find a group near you.

The Compassionate Friends—This organization provides grief support after the loss of a child. Contact The Compassionate Friends at PO Box 3696, Oak Brook, IL 60522; phone: (630) 990-0010 or toll-free (877) 969-0010; or log on to www.compassion atefriends.org.

Survivors of Suicide—This site is designed to help those who have lost a loved one to suicide resolve their grief and pain in their own personal way: http://www.survivorsofsuicide.com.

Endnotes

Chapter 1: The World of Grief

1. Gregory Floyd, *A Grief Unveiled: One Father's Journey Through the Loss of a Child* (Brewster, MA: Paraclete Press, 1999), pp. 116-117.
2. Catherine M. Sanders, Ph.D., *How to Survive the Loss of a Child: Filling the Emptiness and Rebuilding Your Life* (Rocklin, CA: Prima Publishing, 1992, 1998), p. 43.
3. Elizabeth Mehren, *After the Darkest Hour, the Sun Will Shine Again* (New York: Simon & Schuster, Inc., 1997), pp. 145-146.
4. Susan J. Zonnebelt-Smeenge and Robert C. DeVries, *Traveling Through Grief* (Grand Rapids, MI: Baker Publishing Group, 2006), pp. 26-27.
5. Merton P. Strommen, *Five Cries of Grief* (Minneapolis, MN: Augsburg Press, 1996), p. 31.
6. Susan Duke, *Grieving Forward* (New York: Warner, 2006), p. 11.
7. Gerald Sittser, *A Grace Disguised* (Grand Rapids, MI: Zondervan, 1994, 2004), p. 47.
8. Mehren, *After the Darkest Hour,* p. 31.
9. No original source known.
10. Michael Card, *A Sacred Sorrow: Reaching Out to God in the Lost Language of Lament* (Colorado Springs, CO: NavPress, 2005), pp. 30-31.
11. Ibid., p 129.
12. Strommen, *Five Cries of Grief,* adapted.
13. Bob Diets, *Life After Loss* (Tucson, AZ: Fisher Books, 1988), p. 27.
14. Anne Morrow-Lindbergh, *Camp's Unfamiliar Quotations,* p. 124.

Chapter 2: The Need to Grieve

1. J. Shep Jeffreys, *Helping Grieving People* (New York: Brunner-Routledge, 2005), adapted, pp. 31-40.
2. Kim Kluger-Bell, *Unspeakable Losses* (New York: Quill, 2000), p. 44.
3. David and Nancy Guthrie, *When Your Family's Lost a Loved One* (Wheaton, IL: Tyndale House, 2008), p. 5.
4. Ibid., adapted, p. 3.
5. Susan Duke, *Grieving Forward* (New York: Warner, 2006), p. 74.
6. Ibid,, p. 110.
7. Catherine M. Sanders, Ph.D., *How to Survive the Loss of a Child: Filling the Emptiness and Rebuilding Your Life* (Rocklin, CA: Prima Publishing, 1992, 1998), p. 193.
8. Doug Manning, *Don't Take My Grief Away from Me: How to Walk Through Grief and Learn to Live Again* (New York: HarperCollins, 2013), pp. 66-67.
9. Michael Leunig, *A Common Prayer* (New York: HarperCollins, 1991).
10. Susan Duke, *Grieving Forward* (New York: Warner, 2006), pp. 14-15.

Chapter 3: Faces and Feelings of Grief

1. Therese A. Rando, Ph.D., *How to Go On Living When Someone You Love Dies* (New York: Bantam, 1991).
2. Joanne T. Jozefowski, *The Phoenix Phenomenon: Rising from the Ashes of Grief* (Northvale, NJ: Jason Aronson, Inc., 1999, 2001), p. 17.
3. Judy Tatelbaum, *The Courage to Grieve* (New York: HarperPerennial, 1980), p. 28.
4. Ken Gire, *The Weathering Grace of God* (Ann Arbor, MI: Servant Publications, 2001), p. 109.
5. Linda J. Schupp, Ph.D., *Assessing and Treating Trauma and PTSD* (Eau Claire, WI: PESI Healthcare, 2004), p. 3.
6. Thomas Attig, *The Heart of Grief* (New York: Oxford University Press, 2000), p. xi.
7. Ibid., pp. xii, xvi.

Chapter 4: The Death of a Child

1. Catherine M. Sanders, Ph.D., *How to Survive the Loss of a Child* (Rocklin, CA: Prima Publishing, 1992, 1998), p. 17.
2. Judith R. Bernstein, Ph.D., *When the Bough Breaks* (Kansas City, MO: Andrews McMeel Publishing, 1997, 1998), p. 3.
3. Sanders, *How to Survive the Loss of a Child*, p. 9.
4. Elizabeth Mehren, *After the Darkest Hour, the Sun Will Shine Again* (New York: Simon & Schuster, 1997), pp. 97-99.
5. Jennifer L. Buckle and Stephen J. Fleming, *Parenting After the Death of a Child* (New York: Brunner-Routledge, 2010), p. 43.
6. Ibid., pp. 44-45.
7. Ibid., p. 46.
8. Joan Beder, *Voices of Bereavement* (New York: Brunner-Routledge, 2004), adapted, pp. 85-86.
9. Carol Staudacher, *Beyond Grief* (Oakland, CA: New Harbinger, 1987), adapted, pp. 100-101.
10. Therese A. Rando, Ph.D., *Grieving* (Lexington, MA: Lexington Books, 1988), pp. 164-165.
11. Buckle and Fleming, *Parenting After the Death of a Child*, adapted, p. 57.
12. Rando, *Grieving*, adapted, p. 105.
13. Ibid., p. 13.
14. Richard G. Tedeschi and Lawrence G. Calhoun, *Helping Bereaved Parents: A Clinician's Guide* (New York: Brunner-Routledge, 2004), p. 6.
15. Ibid., p. 14.
16. Ann K. Finkbeiner, *After the Death of a Child* (Tampa, FL: Free Press, 1996), p. 4.
17. Ibid., p. 22.
18. Ronald J. Knapp Ph.D., *Beyond Endurance—When a Child Dies* (New York: Schocken, 1986), p. 45.
19. Staudacher, *Beyond Grief*, adapted, p. 109.
20. Barbara D. Rosof, *The Worst Loss* (New York: Henry Holt & Company, 1994), pp. 84-85.
21. Ibid., pp. 77-78.
22. Ibid., adapted.
23. Ibid., pp. 79-80.
24. Knapp, *Beyond Endurance—When a Child Dies*, p. 41.
25. H. Norman Wright, *Recovering from the Losses of Life* (Grand Rapids, MI: Revell, 1991), adapted, pp. 48-49.
26. Knapp, *Beyond Endurance—When a Child Dies*, adapted, p. 184.
27. Ann Kaiser Stearns, *Coming Back* (New York: Ballantine, 1988), p. 172.
28. Knapp, *Beyond Endurance—When a Child Dies*, p. 29.
29. Rando, *Grieving*, adapted, p. 169; Staudacher, *Beyond Grief*, adapted, p. 116.
30. Finkbeiner, *After the Death of a Child*, adapted, p. 104.

31. Judy Carole Kauffmann and Mary Jordan, *The Essential Guide to Life After Bereavement* (Philadelphia, PA: Jessica Kingsley Publishers, 2013).

Chapter 5: Recovering from the Death of a Child

1. Carol Staudacher, *Beyond Grief* (Oakland, CA: New Harbinger, 1987), adapted, pp. 117-118.
2. Therese A. Rando, *Grieving* (Lexington, MA: Lexington Books, 1988), adapted, pp. 177-178.
3. Catherine M. Sanders, Ph.D., *How to Survive the Loss of a Child* (Rocklin, CA: Prima Publishing, 1992), p. 97.
4. Ibid., adapted, pp. 212-214.
5. "Single Parent Grief—After the Loss of a Child," *Bereavement,* Duke University Health System, 2002. http://www.dukehealth.org/repository/dukehealth/ 2005/05/23/09/12/ 48/5648/Child-Single_Parent_Grief.pdf (accessed January 2014).
6. David W. Wiersbe, *Gone, But Not Lost* (Grand Rapids, MI: Baker Books, 1992, 2011), p. 55.
7. Ronald J. Knapp Ph.D., *Beyond Endurance—When a Child Dies* (New York: Schocken, 1986), p. 206.
8. Dr. Ken Garland, professor, Talbot Graduate School of Theology, La Mirada, California. Used by permission.
9. "No More Night," Walt Harrah (Nashville, TN: Word Music, 1983).

Chapter 6: Loss Before and After Birth

1. Kim Kluger-Bell, *Unspeakable Losses* (New York: Quill, 2000), p. 23.
2. Ibid., pp. 20-22.
3. Ibid., p. 26.
4. Donna Gibbs, Becky Garrett, and Phyllis Rabon, *Water from the Rock* (Chicago: Moody Press, 2002), pp. 20-21.
5. Debra Bridwell, *The Ache for a Child* (Colorado Springs, CO: Victor Books, 1994), adapted, pp. 95-103.
6. Ibid., adapted, pp. 94-95.
7. Sandra Glahn and William Cutrer, MD, *When Empty Arms Become a Heavy Burden* (Grand Rapids, MI: Kregal Publications, 2010), p. 76.
8. John DeFrau, "Learning About Grief from Normal Families: SIDS, Stillbirth, and Miscarriage," *Journal of Marital and Family Therapy,* July 1992, adapted, p. 223.
9. Ibid., adapted, p. 229.
10. Therese A. Rando, *Grieving* (Lexington, MA: Lexington Books, 1988), adapted, pp. 181-183.
11. Glahn and Cutrer, MD, *When Empty Arms Become a Heavy Burden,* p. 64.
12. As quoted in Delores Kuenning, *Helping People Through Grief* (Minneapolis, MN: Bethany, 1987), p. 130.
13. Brenda Romanchik, "Birthparent Grief," Adoption.com, 1995, adapted. http://library. adoption.com/articles/birthparent-grief.html (accessed January 2014).
14. Carol Staudacher, *Beyond Grief* (Oakland, CA: New Harbinger, 1987), p. 104.
15. Rando, *Grieving,* adapted, pp. 183-186.
16. Kuenning, *Helping People Through Grief,* p. 63.
17. Ibid., adapted, p. 60.
18. Staudacher, *Beyond Grief,* p. 108.
19. Kuenning, *Helping People Through Grief,* p. 63.
20. Gibbs, Garrett and Rabon, *Water from the Rock,* p. 135.
21. C. S. Lewis, *A Grief Observed* (New York: Bantam, 1961), p. 9.
22. Staudacher, *Beyond Grief,* p. 227.
23. Kluger-Bell, *Unspeakable Losses,* adapted, pp. 137-140.

24. Dale and Juanita Ryan, *Recovery from Loss* (Downers Grove, IL: InterVarsity Press, 1990), adapted, pp. 40-41.

25. Rando, *Grieving*, adapted, pp. 281-283.

26. Ibid., adapted, pp. 284-286.

Chapter 7: The Disabled Child

1. William C. Healey, "Helping Parents Deal with the Fact That Their Child Has a Disability," *LD Online*, 1997, adapted. http://www.ldonline.org/article/Helping_Parents_Deal_with_the_Fact_That_Their_Child_Has_a_Disability?theme=print (accessed January 2014).

2. Robert A. Naseef, Ph.D., *Special Children, Challenged Parents* (Baltimore, MD: Paul Brookes Publishing, 2001), p. 52.

3. Susan Roos, *Chronic Sorrow* (New York, London: Brunner-Routledge, 2002).

4. Naseef, Ph.D., *Special Children, Challenged Parents*, p. xi.

5. Ibid., p. 16.

6. Irving Dickman and Dr. Sol Gordon, *One Miracle at a Time* (New York: Fireside, 1985), n.p.

7. Roos, *Chronic Sorrow*, adapted, pp. 58-59.

8. Ibid., adapted, pp. 64-65.

9. Naseef, Ph.D., *Special Children, Challenged Parents*, p. 249.

10. Dickman and Gordon, *One Miracle at a Time*, pp. 98, 100-101.

11. Helen Featherstone, *A Difference in the Family* (New York: Penguin Books, 1980), pp. 232-233.

12. Roos, *Chronic Sorrow*, p. 122.

13. Ibid., adapted, p. 122.

14. Charlotte E. Thompson, *Raising a Handicapped Child* (New York: Morrow, 1986), adapted, pp. 62-64.

15. Ibid., p. 66.

16. Rando, *Grieving*, pp. 178-179, adapted.

17. Thomas M. Skric, Jean Ann Summers, Mary Jane Brotherson and Ann P. Turnbull, "Severely Handicapped Children and Their Brothers and Sisters," *Severely Handicapped Youth and Their Families* (Orlando Academy, 1984), pp. 215-246. As discussed in Rosemary S. Cook, *Parenting a Child with Special Needs* (Grand Rapids, MI: Zondervan, 1992).

18. Roos, *Chronic Sorrow*, adapted, pp. 116-117.

19. "Birth Defects," Centers for Disease Control and Prevention, July 15, 2013. http://www.cdc.gov/ncbddd/birthdefects/data.html (accessed January 2014).

20. D'Vera Cohen, "U.S. Counts One in 12 Children as Disabled: Census Reflects Increase of Handicapped Youth," *Washington Post*, July 5, 2002, p. BO1.

21. "Birth Defects," Kids Health, June 2010. http://kidshealth.org/parent/system/ill/birth_defects.html (accessed January 2014).

22. Roos, *Chronic Sorrow*, adapted, pp. 87.

23. Dickman and Gordon, *One Miracle at a Time*, p. 109.

24. Ibid., p. 98.

25. Naseef, Ph.D., *Special Children, Challenged Parents*, pp. 161-164.

26. R. Scott Sullender, *Losses in Later Life: A New Way of Walking with God* (New York: Paulist Press, 1989), p. 142.

Chapter 8: The Child Who Disappears

1. Pauline Boss, *Ambiguous Loss* (Cambridge, MA: Harvard University Press, 2000), adapted, pp. 3-9.

2. James Lehman, MSW: "Running Away Part I: Why Kids Do It and How to Stop Them," Empowering Parents. http://www.empoweringparents.com/Runaway-Teens-Why-They-Do-It-and-How-to-Stop-Them.php# (accessed January 2014).
3. "The Ten Reasons Why Children Disappear," Missing Children International. missingchildreninternational.org/articles/ten_reasons_why_children_disappear.html (accessed January 2014).
4. "FAQs: Missing Children," National Center for Missing and Exploited Children. http://www.missingkids.com/Missing/FAQ (accessed January 2014).
5. David Finkelhor, Gerald Hotaling, Andrea Sedlak, *Missing, Abducted, Runaway, and Thrown Away Children in America: First Report*, Washington, DC: U.S. Department of Justice, Office of Juvenile Justice and Delinquency Prevention, May 1990. https://www.ncjrs.gov/pdffiles1/ojjdp/nismart90.pdf (accessed January 2014).
6. Ibid.
7. C. Hatcher, C. Barton, and L. Brooks, *Families of Missing Children*, Final Report to Office of Juvenile Justice and Delinquency Prevention (1992), San Francisco, CA: Center for the Study of Trauma, University of California–San Francisco.
8. Georgia K. Hilgeman, MA, "Impact of Family Child Abduction," *California Child Abduction Task Force* (www.childabductions.org/impact2.html, 5/10/2013).
9. Roberta Rand Caponey, *Responding in Love to an Adult Gay Child*. http://www.focuson thefamily.com/parenting/parenting_roles/parenting-adult-children/responding-in-love-to-an-adult-gay-child.aspx (2002).
10. Ibid.
11. Ibid., adapted.
12. Ibid.
13. Marcia Mitchell, *Surviving the Prodigal Years* (Lynnwood, WA: Emerald Books, 1995), pp. 80-81.
14. Dr. Marie Harwell-Walker, psychologist and marriage and family counselor, "Teens and Drugs: What a Parent Can Do to Help." http://psychcentral.com/lib/teens-and-drugs-what-a-parent-can-do-to-help/000166.
15. Buddy Scott, *Relief for Hurting Parents* (Lake Jackson, TX: Allon Publishing, 1994), p. 12.

Chapter 9: The Loss of a Child Through Trauma

1. Wendy N. Zubenko and Joseph Capozzoli, eds., *Children and Disasters: A Practical Guide to Healing and Recovery* (New York: Oxford University Press, 2002), adapted, p. 99.
2. Debra Whiting Alexander, *Children Changed by Trauma: A Healing Guide* (Oakland, CA: New Harbinger, 1999), p. 5.
3. Ibid., adapted, p. 96.
4. Dave Ziegler, *Traumatic Experience and the Brain* (Phoenix, AZ: Acacia Publishing, 2002), adapted, p. 58.
5. Alexander, *Children Changed by Trauma: A Healing Guide*, adapted, p. 35.
6. Ziegler, *Traumatic Experience and the Brain*, adapted, pp. 42-44.
7. Ibid., adapted, p. 56.
8. Robin Karr-Morse and Meredith S. Wiley, *Ghosts from the Nursery: Tracing the Roots of Violence* (New York: Atlantic Monthly Press, 1997), adapted, pp. 159, 163.
9. Kendall Johnson, *Trauma in the Lives of Children* (Alameda, CA: Hunter House Publishers, 1998), adapted, pp. 46-47.
10. Alexander, *Children Changed by Trauma: A Healing Guide*, adapted, pp. 81-82.
11. Ibid., pp. 25-26.
12. H. Norman Wright, *It's O.K. to Cry: A Parent's Guide to Helping Children Through the Losses of Life* (Colorado Springs, CO: WaterBrook Press, 2004), pp. 195-198.

Chapter 10: Choosing Family Balance

1. Jennifer L. Buckle and Stephen J. Fleming, *Parenting After the Death of a Child* (New York: Routledge, 2011), adapted, pp. 110-112.
2. H. Norman Wright, *Helping Those in Grief* (Ventura, CA: Regal Books, 2011), adapted, pp. 179-192.
3. Gerald Mann, *When the Bad Times Are Over for Good* (Brentwood, TN: Wolgemuth & Hyatt, 1992), p. 169.
4. John Killinger, *For God's Sake, Be Human* (Waco, TX: Word, 1970), p.147, as quoted in Richard Exley, *The Rhythm of Life* (Tulsa, OK: Honor Books, 1992), adapted, p. 168.

Chapter 11: Your Marriage Relationship

1. Jane Brody, *Jane Brody's Guide to the Great Beyond: A Practical Primer to Help You and Your Loved Ones Prepare Medically, Legally and Emotionally for the End of Life* (New York: Random House, 2009), p. 143.
2. Ann Finkbeiner, *After the Death of a Child* (Tampa, FL: Free Press, 1996), adapted, pp. 46, 48.
3. Judith R. Bernstein, Ph.D., *When the Bough Breaks* (Kansas City, MO: Andrews McMeel Publishing, 1997, 1998), adapted, pp. 122-123.
4. Finkbeiner, *After the Death of a Child,* adapted, p. 47.
5. Barbara D. Rosof, *The Worst Loss* (New York: Henry Holt and Company, 1994), adapted, pp. 131-132.
6. Rosemarie S. Cook, *Parenting a Child with Special Needs* (Grand Rapids, MI: Zondervan, 1992), p. 83.
7. Therese A. Rando, *Grieving* (Lexington, MA: Lexington Books, 1988), adapted, pp. 170-171.
8. Bernstein, *When the Bough Breaks,* p. 110.
9. "A Child's Death Changes Everything," Marriage Missions International, Oro Valley, AZ, adapted. http://www.marriagemissions.com/a-childs-death-changes-everything (accessed January 2014).
10. Jean Galicia, MFT, "The Effects of the Loss of a Child on Marriage," adapted. http://www.theravive.com/research/The-Effects-of-the-Death-of-a-Child-on-a-Marriage.
11. Rando, *Grieving,* adapted, pp. 172-173.
12. Galicia, "The Effects of the Loss of a Child on Marriage."
13. Carol Staudacher, *Beyond Grief* (Oakland, CA: New Harbinger, 1987), adapted, p. 123.
14. Galicia, "The Effects of the Loss of a Child on Marriage."
15. Ibid.
16. Rosof, *The Worst Loss,* pp. 97-98.
17. Galicia, "The Effects of the Loss of a Child on Marriage," adapted.
18. Allen Klein, *The Courage to Laugh* (New York: Penguin Putnam, Inc., 1998), n.p.

Chapter 12: The Other Children—Your Response

1. Jennifer L. and Stephen J. Fleming, *Parenting After the Death of a Child* (New York: Brunner-Routledge, 2010), p. 115.
2. Ibid., adapted, pp. 113-123.
3. Ibid., adapted, p. 123.
4. Ibid., p. 118.
5. Ibid., pp. 117-118.
6. Ibid., pp. 141-142.
7. Ibid., adapted, p. 142.
8. Ann K. Finkbeiner, *After the Death of a Child* (Tampa, FL: Free Press, 1996), adapted, p. 67.

9. Gary J. Oliver and H. Norman Wright, *Kids Have Feelings, Too* (Wheaton, IL: Victor Books, 1993), p. 115.
10. Therese Rando, *Grieving* (Lexington, MA: Lexington Books, 1988), adapted, p. 180.

Chapter 13: Grandparents
1. Mary Lou Reed, *Grandparents Cry Twice: Help for Bereaved Grandparents* (Amityville, NY: Baywood Publishing Company, 2000), pp. 21-22.
2. "A Grief Like No Other," *AARP Magazine*, December 2013–June 2014, adapted, p. 54 ff.
3. "The Grief of Grandparents," Loma Linda University Health. http://lomalinda-health.org/medical-center/our-services/bereavement/resources/articles/grandparent-grief.page (accessed January 2014).
4. Ibid.
5. T. A. Rando (ed), *Parental Loss of a Child* (Champaign, IL: Research Press Company, 1986), adapted, pp. 417-418.
6. Ibid., adapted, p. 418.
7. Reed, *Grandparents Cry Twice: Help for Bereaved Grandparents*, adapted, pp. 38-39.
8. Ibid., adapted.
9. Ibid., adapted, p. 59.
10. Ibid., p. 59.
11. Ibid., adapted, p. 58.
12. Pat Schwiebert, RN, *A Grandparent's Sorrow* (Portland, OR: Perinatal Loss/Grief Watch, 1996), pp. 6-7.
13. Marilyn Gryte, RN, MS, "When a Baby Dies, Helping a Family Grieve," Carendalet Management Institute Lecture, Phoenix, AZ, September 17, 1992.
14. Reed, *Grandparents Cry Twice: Help for Bereaved Grandparents*, pp. 95-96.
15. Margaret H. Gerner, *For Bereaved Grandparents* (Omaha, NE: Centering Corp., 2004), adapted, pp. 37-38.
16. "The Grief of Grandparents," Compassionate Friends, 2009, adapted. http://www.compassionatefriends.org/Brochures/the_grief_of_grandparents.aspx (accessed January 2014).
17. Alan Wolfelt, *A Child's View of Grief* (Denver, CO: Companion Press, 2004), p. 28.
18. Reed, *Grandparents Cry Twice: Help for Bereaved Grandparents*, adapted, pp. 87-88.

Other Titles from
H. Norman Wright

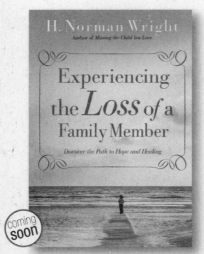

Experiencing the Loss of a Family Member
ISBN: 978.08307.71066

The Complete Guide to Crisis &
Trauma Counseling
ISBN: 978.08307.58401

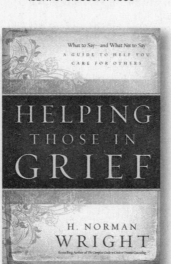

Helping Those in Grief
ISBN: 978.08307.58715

Healing Grace for Hurting People
ISBN: 978.08307.43957

Available wherever books are sold!

Regal
God's Word for Your World™